AWAKE and ALIVE

AWAKE AND ALIVE

Being What You Already Are

MICHAEL HALL, PhD

Binghamton, New York, USA

ISBN 9781700082534

Copyright © 2019 Michael Hall, PhD

All rights reserved. Other than for the purposes and subject to the conditions prescribed under the *Copyright Act*, no part of this publication may be reproduced, stored in a retrieval system, or transmitted in any form or by any means, electronic, mechanical, photocopying, recording or otherwise, without the prior permission of the author.

Disclaimer
This book is intended to be used for educational purposes only. It does not attempt to diagnose or treat any psychological or medical problem. If you believe you need psychological or medical assistance, please consult a qualified practitioner.

Cover photo by Michael Hall, PhD   Used by permission.

Cover design by Lynda Helmer

TABLE OF CONTENTS

Introduction		*1*
One	ARE YOU DEAD OR ALIVE	7
Two	THE NO PATH TO AWAKENING	29
Three	A MIND IS A TERRIBLE PLACE TO BE	51
Four	THE PRACTICE BEFORE AND AFTER AWAKENING	71
Five	SURRENDER SEEKING AND FIND	87
Six	AN INTERNAL PERCEPTUAL SHIFT	103
Seven	DOING WITHOUT A DOER	123
Eight	DAILY LIFE IS THE WAY	135
Nine	OBSTACLES TO AWAKENING	149
Ten	IS SUFFERING DESIRABLE?	163
Eleven	HUMAN BEINGS ARE WANTING MACHINES	175
Twelve	ADDICTIONS ARE US	183
Thirteen	RAINBOWS END	195
Fourteen	MY JOURNEY HOME	207
Acknowledgements		*227*
About the Author		*229*
Glossary		*231*
Resources		*239*
Bibliography		*247*

Dedication

This book is dedicated to all those courageous women and men who recognized the light of awareness and kept it shining in the world. Without the dedicated efforts of so many throughout space and time this work could never have been written. We stand on the shoulders of giants.

Introduction

This is what we speak, not in words taught us by human wisdom/ but in words taught by the Spirit, expressing spiritual truths in spiritual words.

1 Corinthians 2:13

We have forgotten who and what we are. The term awakening has become widely used to mean many different internal experiences. In this book, awakening will refer to an internal perceptual shift that includes the direct, experiential realization of who and what you really are and always have been, that which you can't *not* be. It is a kind of remembrance and recognition of our true nature, underneath all social conditioning and programming. This true nature is universal, unchanging, and equally available to all at any time or place.

With a genuine and abiding awakening, a new way of perceiving the world spontaneously arises. Awakening is an internal perceptual shift of enormous importance. In this new manner of perceiving, people and things are known directly as they are, not as we believe they are, think they should be, or wish they were. Seeing occurs no longer with only the eyes, but with the entire being. In this book, the seeing that emerges naturally following this experience is called *clear seeing*. Life is seen directly as it is, with less obscuring that can result from the beliefs, programs, and conditioning of the ordinary mind. Intuition is heightened, and as such we know information we could not possibly know. Understandings and realizations about how things work become readily apparent without any noticeable effort on our part. Life lives itself, with minimal interference from preconceptions and inaccurate assumptions. Everything has a natural rhythm and flow, with little to no interference. The awareness that arises is direct and unmediated. It is not dependent on language or thought. In the Zen Buddhist tradition, it is called no-mind awareness. This no-mind awareness is explicitly referred to in other major religious traditions, which I discuss in this book, including various schools of Buddhism, Christianity, and the Advaita Vedanta schools of Hinduism. No-mind awareness is implied in Judaism and Islam, but I am not as familiar with those teachings and will not refer to them as frequently in this book.

The internal experience of this clear seeing is a lack of interest in creating problems, difficulties, and interpersonal drama. Life becomes infinitely easier and more enjoyable. Life is not problem-free because everyone retains to some degree a residual attachment to programmed beliefs, opinions, and assumptions.

The goal of this book is to help you clear out the mental and emotional debris that obstructs your ability to know reality directly for yourself. All that you need to know is continuously revealed. Life supports you in an infinite number of ways both visible and invisible. Every sincere effort you make is valuable to yourself and all beings. You cannot fail at this work. Have faith in your own ability to see the truth of your being. We all benefit immeasurably from the efforts of those who have gone before us.

Different teachers and methods resonate with different individuals. No teacher or path fits everyone. I recommend you form a strong intention to awaken in this lifetime for the benefit of yourself and all beings. Along with this passionate intention, an accurate understanding of the path, along with trust and surrender are all that are needed. Trust especially your inner intuitive sense of what is best for you at a given time.

All aspects of your life begin to change as you progress along this path. You find that others become much easier to get along with as you begin to lose interest in judging and evaluating them. People often believe that unexpressed thoughts of a critical nature have no bearing on relationships. However, with increasing awareness and acceptance of reality it becomes clear that unconscious or suppressed thoughts, judgments, and feelings *do* have an energetic reality of their own. When we deconstruct the beliefs and assumptions that lead to angry or entitled thoughts and feelings, our energetic presence becomes calmer and more peaceful. Without critical thoughts and feelings life becomes considerably easier and more pleasant for others and for us. As we lose interest in defending our own programming and conditioning, our family and friends will find us more enjoyable and appealing. It becomes easier for others to let their guard down around us as they no longer need to protect themselves in our presence.

Forgiveness and compassion arise spontaneously with our commitment and intention to change ourselves instead of trying to change others. Our intention should always be to turn inward. Relentless self-awareness and self-responsibility are our main tools. Self-acceptance is necessary for real change to occur. It is much more sensible to try to change what we can change. We can always change our own perspective. Changing external realities may or may not be possible. This book is a manual of how to live in accordance with the world as it is, not as we wish it were or believe it should be.

Learning to live comfortably in our own skin may not sound like a lofty spiritual goal, but why not begin there? Real inner peace can come only from the welcoming embrace of everything exactly as it is, with nothing and no one left out or excluded. This perspective is radically inclusive. Can we welcome all that we are, rejecting nothing, appreciating the gift of this life as it is, without needing it to be different? Can we learn to accept ourselves as we are now, without automatically assuming we are somehow inadequate, insufficient, or flawed? Can we apply the same radical acceptance to everyone we meet, and to all that is? Ceaselessly wanting more of this and less of that is a recipe for more of the same disappointment and despair that most of us already know too well. A radical break is needed from our deeply conditioned, robot-like life.

This book is designed to teach you about direct, no-mind awareness and its manifestation in ordinary life. The teachings of this book cannot be realized in the same manner that we would learn chemistry or a foreign language. A different kind of learning is required to make some sense of the ideas proposed here.

The place to start is where you are right now. Begin by reading and absorbing this book with your thinking mind. This logical, rational level of understanding is, at best, a jumping-off point. *Real* understanding occurs on its own through a kind of intuitive resonance. It cannot be forced but emerges organically and at the right time. Repetition is key to this new way of understanding. Repeated absorption helps the developmental process naturally unfold.

It took me many years as a practicing clinical psychologist to accept that real change happens gradually and only when the time is ripe. I encourage you to allow repetition to function as a deepening process. What is most important is that you persist. Return to difficult passages in this book as often as you need. Many of these ideas may be new to you. Real understanding comes from steeping yourself in these ideas without the pressure to grasp quickly what may be unfamiliar. When you read an idea that you do not understand, try to relax, breathe, and let go. The ordinary thinking mind cannot comprehend the material contained in this book. Once experiential understanding arises spontaneously on its own, everything will seem very clear.

I hope this book encourages you to question deeply the beliefs and assumptions that you previously accepted without awareness, thought, comment, or protest. A rich and meaningful life is your birthright. What is stopping you from living your life right now? Look deeply into all perceived obstacles and you will find nothing but more programmed beliefs and assumptions, all of which are fundamentally false. None are needed to live free in this world as it is.

Reflect for a moment on the beautiful lines of the 23rd Psalm:

You prepare a table before me in the presence of my enemies;
You anoint my head with oil; my cup overflows.

Surely your goodness and love will follow me all the days of my life,
and I will dwell in the House of the LORD forever.

The feast of your life is given freely, laid out before you. It is not necessary to earn or deserve it. Simply seize what is rightfully yours.

Can you savor and enjoy each morsel, exactly as it is, needing nothing to be different?

Chapter One

ARE YOU DEAD OR ALIVE?

The spontaneous realization of our true nature is impossible to accurately describe. Often it is expressed as the direct, experiential realization of the fundamental emptiness, nothingness, or void that underlies all apparent phenomena. Everything that has always appeared to be solid, substantial, or enduring is recognized as merely an artifact of perception. One way this truth occurred to me is the intuitive recognition that there is no place solid or substantial to stand anywhere in the universe. Everything that appears to be real is not actually real in the way we have understood it to be. This direct realization is not an intellectual construct or belief. Rather, it is a direct knowing that reveals itself in a way that cannot be doubted or questioned.

If nothing whatsoever is real, solid, substantial, or enduring in the way we have been taught, then who am I? The *I* that has appeared to be *me* is recognized as merely a construct or conditioned belief. The inner sense of a continuous, real, substantial, or enduring self-identity is true in a way, just not true in the way we believe. Everything exists because we perceive it to exist and for no other reason. Nothing exists *out there*. It all exists, to the extent that it does, *in here* in my inner perceptual world which I create, guided by my conditioned beliefs and assumptions, in a moment to moment manner. From the Absolute or no-mind perspective, in here and out there are not two. This truth was revealed to me experientially, but I have since found contemporary scientists who have come to the same realization using the methods of scientific research.

From my own experiential realizations as well as the literature on awakening, I identify six distinct components of awakening. These components represent different aspects of the complete awakening phenomena, which may emerge together all at once, or may arise somewhat separately and over an extended period of time. They can occur in any order. These six elements are: 1) Emptiness; 2) Oneness; 3) Dissolution of self-identity; 4) Spontaneous action arising from no-mind awareness; 5) Rebirth as a new being; and 6) Presence awareness.

I will now briefly describe each of these components.

1) Emptiness: Equivalent terms you will read are the void, no-mind awareness, the Absolute, Nondual awareness, true nature, Mind, and the Self. Emptiness is described in the following words of the Heart Sutra: *Form is only emptiness, emptiness only form. Form is no other than emptiness, emptiness no other than form.* My first real awakening experience in 1982 was apparently triggered by reading these words. The words of the Heart Sutra express the very core of the Mahayana Buddhist teachings of Zen and Tibetan Buddhism. The direct, experiential realization of the truth of these words is called awakening because it is as if you suddenly woke up from a deep sleep. Everything, including yourself, is seen for the first time through fresh eyes and without the distortion of cultural programming and conditioning. With this direct, personal realization, there is no going back. Nothing changes and everything changes. Nothing will ever again be the same, yet in an equally valid way, nothing is different. In describing this realization, paradox cannot be avoided and is not a problem to the awakened mind. It is virtually impossible for our regular thinking mind to comprehend two contradictory truths simultaneously. This is one very important reason why the ordinary mind cannot grasp the truths revealed by no-mind awareness.

Strangely, the emptiness of all phenomena is not empty. The emptiness described in Buddhist teachings is full, just not full of *things*. Nothing is separate or outside this primordial emptiness which contains and transcends what is and what is not. We are this emptiness, yet we simultaneously exist in a unique form, in a unique body and mind, and in a unique time and place. Both are simultaneously true.

2) Oneness: A second component to awakening is the experiential realization of oneness or lack of separation or differentiation regarding all things. While we are not the same as everything, we are not fundamentally different either. This recognition is the root of genuine compassion, acceptance, and forgiveness. Emptiness underlies the lack of difference. Oneness underlies the lack of sameness.

All spiritual teachings from the perspective of awakened awareness include both the form aspect of reality and the emptiness aspect. Everything is the same, yet at the same time all is unique and different. In authentic spiritual teaching, there is a continuous play with the paradox of form and emptiness. Seemingly contradictory answers may be given to what appears to be the same question asked by different individuals at different times and under different circumstances. From the perspective of a spiritual teacher, is the student currently stuck in form or in emptiness? Is this ordinary world too real, or not real enough?

3) Dissolution of self-identity: Another component of awakening is the partial or complete dissolution of our self-identity. This self-identity is a perception of the *me* that is born and dies. It was always taken for granted and assumed to be real without question. Who gets up in the morning? I do. Who plans a vacation? I do. After self-realization, the awareness is that *something* gets out of bed and plans a vacation. Yet, it is impossible to say what that something is. It just

is. This something that activates the body and mind is no longer perceived to be the self I previously perceived myself to be. Nor is it a thing or entity of any sort. I call it awareness. Awareness gets up in the morning. Awareness plans a vacation. Awareness speaks and acts or Awareness chooses not to. There is absolutely no one in charge. There is no sense of individual volition. Things simply happen the way they do. Or they don't. If this doesn't make sense to you, that is just fine. It won't make sense until you have had a similar shift in internal perspective.

With awakening self-identity dissolves either partially or completely, all at once or progressively over time. The loss of identification with one's historic body and mind has been noted by all awakened teachers and in all scriptures. In *The Ashtavakra Gita* it is said:

> *Abide in Awareness*
> *with no illusion of person.*
> *You will be instantly free and at peace.*
>
> Marshall, B., 2009, p. 95

The distinguishing characteristics of this experiential realization of our essential nature have been expressed in remarkably similar ways for thousands of years. There is nothing new in what I am sharing, yet the expression of emptiness through an individual is always fresh and original.

If all is fundamentally empty and void, it is obvious that our self-identity is nothing more than a convenient fiction not to be taken too seriously. The loss of interest in the constructed self-identity creates a tremendous sense of liberation, as there is no longer a need to protect or defend this largely imaginary social fiction. It becomes gradually and progressively easier to see the world as it is rather than as we believe it should be. The ability to see things as they are and accept what *is* expands exponentially with the diminution of our self-identity.

4) Spontaneous action arising from no-mind awareness: Another characteristic of awakening pivotal in the Zen Buddhist tradition is the ability to manifest experientially and behaviorally through spontaneous thought and action the understanding described above. Throughout this book I will describe this free and spontaneous behavior as thinking, speaking and acting from no-mind awareness. A purely conceptual understanding is not enough. Merely reporting an awakening experience to a Zen master, no matter how profound and transformative, would not be accepted as a real awakening. It is necessary to demonstrate the understanding on demand in life and action in a one-on-one interview with a Zen master to show that understanding has penetrated deeply enough to be embodied in behavior.

Show me your new understanding might be a typical injunction from a Zen master to a student new to this world of emptiness. This pure awareness is called *no-mind* because it does not have its origin in thought, although it may manifest as thought. This direct, unmediated awareness is universal, impersonal, and not constrained by anyone's body or mind. Yet it always manifests in the world *through* a body and mind.

5) Rebirth as a new being: This rebirth entails the perception of biological changes in the body consistent with the idea of being born again. In addition to changes in cognition and perception, awakening is a deeply biological phenomenon. It seems as if the body is radically different at a cellular level, although there appears to be no scientific proof of this. Still, all kinds of side effects and fallout may manifest biologically as the body-mind adapts and learns to embody this radical alteration in perception and understanding.

6) Presence awareness: This component of awakening relates to the experience of being fully present in each moment. Much has been written about the transformative effects of awakening. Far less has been written about the embodiment of this enduring no-mind awareness. To live out this emptiness in our body in the world seems to be a much harder process than the direct realization of emptiness. Being fully present in each moment of our life transforms our relationship to other people and to any activity in which we might engage. The inner experience of the state of presence can be described as dwelling in the presence of God. It is felt to be a kind of bliss that is empty of mental content, whole and complete, lacking nothing, desiring nothing, avoiding nothing.

Throughout the book I will continue to describe and explore these various components of awakening, often as parts of an integrated whole as lived in everyday life. As you read these descriptions, please reflect on your own experiences as I believe you may have more familiarity with these phenomena than you currently realize.

Common Misunderstandings about Awakening

The great Japanese Zen master Hakuin once noted that he had 17 great awakenings and hundreds of minor ones. Hakuin continued Zen practice to both deepen and further embody his realization. He lived in a culture and spiritual tradition in which there was a profound respect for the infinite varieties and degrees of awakening and its embodiment by a human being. In the West, we love to simplify, ignore nuance, and cut to the chase. We also like to assume an egalitarian mindset, which avoids judgment or discrimination. Yet it is obvious that all awakenings are not created equal. Many people I have met have experienced a brief, fleeting, fragmentary glimpse of the emptiness aspect of awakening and assume they have finished this great work. There are infinite levels of awakening. A brief glimpse is not the same as a deeply embodied, abiding no-mind awareness that is continuously manifest in thought and behavior. Many years of sustained practice are necessary after even the deepest awakening to fully embody the new realizations.

I also noticed the tendency to believe that with a genuine awakening you wake up once and for all, and that you are then finished with no more work to be done. Nothing could be further from the truth. Given these two prevalent misunderstandings, what are we to make of Hakuin's statement when some current teachers claim that they woke up at a moment in time and then are done, denying the need to integrate, work through, or even embody their realization? What would Hakuin think if he wandered into today's spiritual marketplace free-for-all where there is no quality control, and everyone decides for themselves if they are awakened or not?

Leaving the Cave of Nonduality

Having endured the enormous hardships, turmoil, confusion, and generalized pain and suffering usually necessary for us to be able to see through the veil of conditioning, it is very hard to believe that there could be more. Awakening feels like the death of the old being and the birth of a new one. It takes enormous biological, psychological, and psychic energy for this transformation to occur. Afterwards, there is a tremendous sense of exhilaration, relief, and joy. There is a necessary period of rest and recovery after this epic struggle. However, eventually the energy will arise to begin the process of integration and embodiment of the paradoxical nature of reality. There will be a natural movement forward in our journey towards understanding how to live in this similar yet wholly different world that we now inhabit with varying degrees of conditioning and programming still in place. The challenge becomes learning to live in the world without our fixed self-identity, but with potentially many of the programmed trappings of this identity still intact.

There is a huge temptation to remain resting in the blissful stillness of the Absolute, which I call the Cave of Nonduality. If we remain stuck there, we will believe that nothing else is valuable or worthwhile. Reintegration with ordinary life means coming to terms with the preoccupation with the trivial and routine interpersonal conflicts that are characteristic of the normal, un-awakened mind. Periodic withdrawal into silence and from the demands and responsibilities of everyday life is beneficial as we learn to negotiate living with this new awareness. Yet, we must guard against becoming attached to the peace and stillness of this withdrawal as it can become an obstacle to further realization.

For some the experience of this Cave of Nonduality is timeless emptiness, nothingness, devoid of any feelings. The direct experience of emptiness is often an emotional flatness. This is not at all the same as the psychological defense mechanisms of emotional numbing, avoidance, or dissociation. Rather, it is the result of no longer being able to stir the emotional pot by investing energy in meaningless trivia. So much of what we believed previously to be of critical importance we now recognize to be of no significance. It is difficult or impossible to automatically jump on the bandwagon for or against anything. Shakespeare's Macbeth glimpses this emptiness:

> *Life's but a walking shadow, a poor player*
> *That struts and frets his hour upon the stage*
> *And then is heard no more. It is a tale*
> *Told by an idiot, full of sound and fury.*
> *Signifying nothing.*
>
> Macbeth, Act 5, scene 5,19-28

Some degree of emotional non-reactivity seems characteristic of this post-awakening reorientation. For others, there may be continuous feelings of bliss and joy. It is easy, even natural, to become addicted to the quiet peace of emptiness and the joy of nonattachment. Finally, relieved of a lifetime of anxious, needless worry about actual or perceived loss, we could hardly be blamed for luxuriating in the ability to be present to the myriad small miracles of daily life.

It may be hard to consider letting go of this bliss-filled and peaceful existence and venturing out into the hectic activity of the everyday world. The effortless experience of presence can still be fragile and easily shaken by the confusing and complicated demands of daily life and human interaction. Yet, to journey further requires a willingness to allow life to place us in exactly those situations which stimulate the emergence and working through of our remaining blind spots. This natural movement happens on its own if we have surrendered deeply enough to allow it. Welcoming difficulties as further opportunities to deepen our understanding is the perfect perspective to adopt. Hanging on to the bliss of emptiness is simply a detour on this path. To dwell continually in the emptiness of the Absolute without simultaneously embracing the world of form is to get lost in the quiet, still Cave of Nonduality.

Jonah's Awakening – The Enormous Struggle

At one point not long after my own abiding awakening in 2002, I had a spontaneous direct-seeing of myself. I was lying on the wet, sandy shore of a body of water. I was curled up in the fetal position, naked, shivering from cold and exhaustion, yet strangely content, relieved, and exhilarated. The awareness came that I had been spewed out of the mouth of a whale only moments earlier. There was the sense of a long, dark, timeless struggle in the belly of the whale. How and why I was finally thrown up was unclear, but I was profoundly grateful. It was as if I had been a fur ball in the whale's belly that it had finally tossed out. Completely exhausted, I could not move or even lift my head; I was just panting, alive, free, and utterly spent.

The Biblical story of Jonah (Jonah, 12:10) immediately came to mind, and I was then able to grasp the deeper meaning of Jonah's epic struggle in the belly of the whale. The story has been interpreted as describing the importance of obedience to God's commands. Jonah is directed by God to go to the city of Nineveh and *preach against it, because its wickedness has come up before me* (Jonah, 1:2). Instead, Jonah *ran away from the Lord* (Jonah, 1:3) and boards a ship. God then sends a great storm to the ship. Jonah recognizes his responsibility for this storm as punishment for disobeying God's commands. He volunteers to be thrown overboard, which the other sailors eventually do in fear for their own lives. God helpfully provides a whale to promptly swallow him and prevent drowning.

There are many valuable layers to explore in this story, but the primary interest for now is Jonah's experience once swallowed by the whale. For three days and nights, Jonah is in the pit of the beast, making good use of his time there as he could surrender completely to the will of God. God commands the fish to vomit Jonah onto dry land. Jonah awakens to his true nature. The understanding that the story of Jonah is a metaphor for spiritual awakening was revealed to me by no-mind awareness. Jonah's difficulties in the Biblical story are the direct result of his refusal to follow the will of God. A real awakening can occur only when our will is surrendered to the will of God. This surrender may seem voluntary in the story with Jonah's statement: *What I have vowed I will make good* (Jonah, 2:9), but the depth of surrender required cannot be only a voluntary effort. The self-centered ego can never truly surrender itself. This fundamental truth is noted in Jonah's final comment: *Salvation comes from the Lord* (Jonah, 2:9).

This story represents the archetypal struggle we all face to surrender our will to the will of the Divine. In this report of Jonah's self-transcendence, God is made to appear separate from and outside of Jonah. As I have noted, there is nothing separate from or outside of our true nature. We are always one with the will of God, whether we realize this or not. The appearance of separation is the result of the self's delusional pretense that the self exists as an independent entity separate from God.

Neither Dual nor Nondual

> *Everyday life fits the absolute as a box and its lid.*
> *The absolute and relative work together like two arrows meeting in mid-air.*
>
> The Harmony of Relative and Absolute (Sandokai), Chants and Recitations, p.33.

A major stumbling block for the ordinary thinking mind is accurately understanding the paradoxical nature of the Relative or Dual and the Absolute or Nondual. All major spiritual traditions such as Zen, Tibetan Buddhism and traditional Advaita Vedanta that have incorporated awakening as a central aspect of their teaching recognize that although there are many levels of awakening, there are no levels to emptiness. While no-mind awareness itself does not have levels, the manifestation and embodiment of this awareness at a particular time, in a particular culture, and in a particular body-mind with its own unique history and lineage is subject to infinite degrees of realization and embodiment. Ordinary ways of thinking and perceiving may deny the truth of the Absolute or Nondual, which is without degrees, unchanging, birthless and deathless. Conversely, much of current non-dual teachings appear to deny the Relative or Dual with their insistence that real-world problems do not exist, such as extreme poverty, racism, sexism, climate desecration, and so forth.

The seeming contradiction and paradoxical nature of the Relative and Absolute perspectives progressively diminish as the Nondual realization becomes embodied. Fully integrated awakening transcends the Absolute or Nondual and the Relative or Dual while not denying either one. This unfettered, fully embodied awareness moves freely in the world without concern or disdain for either. This freedom in motion knows neither before nor after which is Nondual, but shows up on time for appointments, which is Dual. For the eventual transcendence of form and emptiness to occur, it is necessary to thoroughly integrate the nondual realization into the duality of daily life.

Some conditioned programming may weaken or largely disappear in the moment and immediate aftermath of awakening. Other issues will remain. While some of these other issues may gradually dissipate over time through the normal processes of living, other issues may not. This is one very important reason that major spiritual traditions caution against teaching or even discussing one's awakening until this new no-mind awareness has been thoroughly embodied. While this process is open-ended, it can take five to ten years or more to marinate and stabilize in an individual. It is important that the individual makes an active effort to see through remaining blocks that obstruct direct awareness from operating freely in and through the body-mind.

The goal is to move freely and skillfully in the relative world once the Absolute is realized. The enduring, experiential realization of the Absolute is not the end of the path. In many ways, it is the beginning. The embodiment of nondual awareness has three major components or aspects representing the mind, the body and the emotions. This realization of the Absolute must be embodied and manifest in all three.

Even with a deep, embodied, nondual realization, which is still quite rare, it is a mistake to assume that all psychological and biological problems disappear. Deeply realized beings do not become omniscient. Nor do they suddenly become skilled and knowledgeable psychologists who can ably assist others with any personal problems. Ongoing problems with the body generally continue. Someone who is diabetic or suffers bipolar disorder before having an awakening will generally continue to have these challenges afterwards.

A few years ago, I attended two five-day silent retreats with a well-known spiritual teacher for whom I have enormous respect. Virtually every question asked by the large audience was psychological in nature. The questions were about coping with illness, loss, addictions, codependency, grieving, anger, dysfunctional relationships with lovers, children, or parents, terror of intimacy, chronic physical or emotional pain, and so forth. I do not remember a single question about awakening or spiritual practice. This felt odd.

From a pure nondual perspective, there are no blocks to awareness, nor is there a person to imagine that they have such blocks. Therefore, it is not necessary or even possible to pay attention to these imaginary blocks which never existed except in the mind and the mind's misunderstanding of reality. All psychological problems, bad habits, addictions, and so forth are dismissed as the province of an imaginary character that is not real and does not require attention. At the level of the nondual, this perspective is accurate. Nothing is real, including who and what we think we are. From the equally valid perspective of duality, such notions are transparent nonsense.

Living freely and spontaneously in the ordinary world is the full embodiment of this awakened awareness. A fully embodied awakening is the personal experience of being alive, awake, and present in this world as it is. Emerging from the dream of our life allows us to see what is real, moment-to-moment, and to act in a direct, free, and spontaneous manner. To awaken to who and what we are and to fully embody that awakened awareness is to live in reality, seeing yourself and others as we are. Living in reality is the goal and purpose of our existence.

Accurately recognizing and accepting reality is the only way we can live at peace in this world. Self-transformation at the deepest level is the way to be at peace with ourselves and others. We will find peace in this world when *we* are at peace.

When speaking and acting out of this embodied no-mind awareness, our words and actions carry unusual power because of their source. We all have ready access to this source that never leaves us. This original source has been called many different names, all pointing to the same underlying reality. This source is who we are long before we are born into this human mind and body and continues unchanged after we have physically died. It will always be with us because it *is* us, unchanging, still, ever-present. This source is eternal and ever present. It is neither born nor does it die. It does not come or go. It cannot be described, although it is continually available to be experienced directly. All notions and concepts describing it are inadequate, inaccurate, and superfluous, yet it can be communicated. It can be demonstrated and expressed in behavior and words, just not explained in ways that our rational, thinking mind can understand. To understand it is to *become* it, to realize what you have always been but seemed to forget in a kind of self-amnesia. In this self-remembering, we become like the prodigal son of the New Testament who was lost but now is found. Returning to his true home, he is instantly recognized by his father.

This underlying, ever present ground of our being is known in Zen Buddhism as our original face before our parents are born. To use the language of Christianity, we can't fall out of the grace of God. We cannot lose who we are. Nor can we find it. This primordial ground of being is beautifully described in the opening lines of the Gospel of John (1:1): *In the beginning was the Word, and the Word was God.*

Learning to recognize and appreciate reality is to see things as they are. When perceiving and acting from our ordinary conditioned awareness, we see only what we have been programmed to see. Yet, we already are so intimately connected to the source of all that is that there are not two; the source and the self are not two, not even one. The Father and Son are not two, not even one. There is just one, and ultimately not even one.

It is nearly impossible to know what is real, as that requires stepping outside of our programming. This programming is continuous and relentless. No one escapes it. Yet it is possible to see *through* our conditioning and grasp directly for ourselves what is true at any given moment. When we realize and fully embody our true nature, it is as if scales have fallen from our eyes and we can finally see what has always been right in front of us but was never noticed.

Seeing clearly what is real allows us gradually to release our culturally conditioned fantasies and delusions. While awakening is always spontaneous and immediate, the progressive disappearance of conditioning occurs over time. It is rarely if ever complete at the time of the original awakening, regardless of the depth or pervasiveness of the realization. This gradual erosion of remaining conditioned blind spots represents the embodiment and manifestation of the no-mind awakened awareness.

Reality Is Always Right

Fight reality and you lose. Fight reality and you suffer. Embrace reality and you walk freely through life undisturbed. When we are truly alive, we begin to see reality as it is, not as we wish it were or think it should be.

Reality never needs to be any different from what it is. Seeing reality as it is and accepting it is the basis of wisdom. This understanding has no similarity to passive resignation. Skillful, effective action in the world is possible only when we see things as they are. Until we learn to see clearly, our ability to be content and peaceful is limited, almost nonexistent.

Without realizing it, most of us see *through a glass, darkly*. As the Apostle Paul says in 1 Corinthians 13:12, *Now we see but a poor reflection as in a mirror; then we shall see face to face*. When natural, clear seeing emerges spontaneously through undeserved grace, you will be able to determine for yourself what is real and what is not.

We are all intricately interconnected. In clear seeing, our ordinary illusion of independence and autonomy is shattered. In the world's spiritual literature, this cessation of the illusion of a separate self is a kind of death. This is not the biological death of the human body, but a spiritual death and rebirth as a new being. This is the true meaning of the frequently misused phrase of *born again*. It is only after this spiritual death and rebirth that we can recognize our oneness with what is. We experience this recognition of who and what we really are as profoundly liberating.

With spiritual death and rebirth, we become able to recognize and value what is real. It is only after this spiritual death and rebirth that we can be one with what *is* rather than with our fantasies, wishful thinking and mistaken illusions.

Reality Is Your Friend

The path of awakening is the path to becoming an actual human being. Becoming a mature human being is an enormous accomplishment, something we must struggle for and strive to achieve. The process is very like our biological birth, full of uncertainty, fear, and trembling. Birth is never easy and requires heroic and persistent effort. Although liberation is ultimately through the action of grace, we must strive to liberate ourselves, by our own efforts, from the universal myths and delusions we are programmed to believe are true.

Our goal is to learn to see clearly and recognize reality in our daily lives. Reality provides infinite resources and support once we commit to the struggle to become fully alive-to become who we already are and can't not be. Realization creates the ability to live with peace and contentment in the real world. None of this work is easy, although there's nothing more important for a human being to accomplish.

One person opening the mind's eye makes it significantly easier for all who come after to do so. Upon his great awakening, Shakyamuni Buddha reportedly said: *When I awoke, all beings awoke with me.* Each person who awakens opens the door a crack for everyone else. For me this is the ultimate meaning of Jesus forgiving the sins of the world as noted in John 1:29:

> *The next day he (John the Baptist) saw Jesus coming to him and said, 'Behold, the Lamb of God who takes away the sin of the world!'*

This is obviously not a traditional interpretation of Christian teaching. In every example mentioned in this book, my interpretation of Biblical passages comes not primarily from learning or study but from direct revelation. This does not mean that my often unusual perspective on the meaning of some Biblical verses is correct on every level. However, I have learned to refrain from second guessing what is directly revealed to me. At the least I hope the perspectives offered throughout this book may provide an alternative interpretation of often confusing passages that may be helpful. I am always listening for the underlying meaning of Biblical stories and attempting to relate important passages to my own direct experience. I encourage you to do the same.

We gain nothing beneficial until we challenge and question our most cherished convictions. You have found this book in your hands, and as such you are ready to begin this serious work. Trust and respect your own direct knowing which has always been present and can never be lost. Have faith in your deepest intuition and instincts about your spiritual journey.

Traditional early Buddhist doctrine teaches the concept of a *stream enterer*, the first stage of enlightenment. This is someone who is not only dedicated to the spiritual path but has also developed some intuitive understanding of the truth. This is the same stream in which John the Baptist baptizes Jesus (Matthew 3:13).

Once no-mind awareness begins to stir, there is no going back. We will never again be satisfied with the superficial pleasures of ordinary life. The pursuit of realization develops a life of its own. The search continues in what is the most appropriate manner for us. We no longer need to be concerned about the results of our practice. We simply recall what is ultimately true, then persist and persevere. The ultimate resolution of this search is to be able to say with the Apostle Paul (Galatians 2:20): *I no longer live, but Christ lives in me.*

The Story of My Awakening

> *Japanese Red Maple*
> *Sun freckled maple*
> *Red canopy. What do you see?*
> *Days turn into years*

Wednesday, September 18, 2002 the *I* that perceived the world as I had known it to be fell away completely. As of the date of this writing, it has not returned.

On that September day, I was sitting in my psychotherapy office with a two-hour break between clients. I picked up *Power vs. Force*, the seminal book on consciousness and spirituality by Dr. David Hawkins. As I was reading the book a spontaneous, instantaneous change occurred, a change so radical and complete that I found it impossible to describe. It was as if at that exact moment I became a biologically different person; in some ways the same, yet in other ways completely original and brand new.

What appears to have happened was the instantaneous disappearance of the illusion of a separate and unique *me* that had a history and existed in time and space. The internal sense of myself that I had found to be consistent and reliable prior to this experience, completely ceased without notice. The world continued as it had before, but now *I* was experiencing it in a brand-new way.

Physically I looked the same, my behavior remained generally the same, and I continued to go to work, but I had undergone an almost impossible to describe internal change. I could no longer identify a reason for why I did anything. Experiencing this radical, perceptual shift was liberating, but also quite puzzling. It would take years for me to reach a point where I could clearly articulate my experience of this internal change.

From the first moment that I experienced this spontaneous internal change, I began using the previously unfamiliar word *grace* to describe what happened to me. Until that moment, the word grace was not a part of my vocabulary. Yet, through the experience of this radical shift, I came to understand that there is an incontrovertible knowing that grace is not earned or deserved. Grace is a gift given to us freely. The profound realization of that fact elicited in me a deep sense of humility and gratitude, both of which I continue to feel to this day.

It usually takes many months or years to be able to speak coherently and helpfully about this radical shift in perception, and I was reminded of that fact when, in those first months after this experience, I tried to share what had happened to me with others.

I Won't Say; I Won't Say

On that September day, I had a break of several hours in my work schedule, so I drove home and babbled to my partner about what had just happened to me. She looked horrified as I explained that I no longer cared about anything. She took this comment rather personally as almost anyone would. I knew what I meant. I just couldn't say it in an articulate or compassionate manner.

This *not caring* was completely impersonal and had nothing to do with her, yet I'm sure it felt very personal to her. I had come to realize that caring as we usually understand it has far more to do with codependency, fear of abandonment, and the need to control the other than anything genuinely loving, considerate or respectful. Caring in the usual sense often creates relationships that are sticky, manipulative, and dishonest. Most of what we usually call caring is a disguised attempt to protect the emotional attachments that our ego treasures and believes necessary for emotional or physical survival. However, I could not articulate all this at that time. The direct experience itself and the ability to describe and convey it are two different events. The realization is always instantaneous. The ability to convey the realization in words that are useful to others takes a long time to evolve and mature.

I had similar experiences with good friends when I tried to describe this new continuous awareness. Shakyamuni Buddha wisely advised those newly arrived in the awareness of *all that is* to remain silent about it for an extended time. Born again in this new and very real way, we are like an orphan without a father or mother. We feel homeless, yet free and radiantly alive in this new space, this new place. We have no more questions to ask or answers to seek. We gradually become aware, however, of a new and different type of aloneness. In my case, I had previously had this experience but had never been able to identify it. This aloneness was not painful, yet it was poignant to grasp the concept that it would no longer be possible to unconsciously participate in the cherished illusions of normal life in the way that to me had once been so natural and effortless.

We experience this new awareness in our physical body, and our body must change biologically to accommodate this new awareness. The nervous system needs quiet and often some degree of protection from ordinary life. With time and self-reflection, awareness is gradually embodied in all aspects of daily living. Understanding slowly arises both conceptually and intuitively as the mind and body marinate in this new way of seeing, knowing and acting.

In many important ways, we are not in charge of our lives. Certainly, we cannot make a genuine awakening occur. It happens when and if it happens, and is always a profound, unfathomable gift.

Prior to September 18, 2002, I had four previous awakening experiences of varying depths. The first occurred in 1965 at the very end of my first year in college. This incomplete but compelling experience launched my serious spiritual search. The other three experiences happened in the early 1980s, within the context of my study and practice of Zen Buddhism. All were extremely important and transformative, serving to further alter my previous view of the world. Yet these unique and very different experiences were limited in that they were temporary. Although with each one I experienced a significant and liberating change in perception, the change was transient, and I still struggled with the problem of being *me*.

What happened in 2002 was unlike the four previous awakenings I had experienced. Thus, it is difficult to describe. I now refer to what happened in 2002 as a cessation or ending, a no longer coming into being. My self-identity, the self-centered, endlessly narcissistic and fearful *I* ended, yet everything continued exactly as before. Over time, it became clear to me that the awareness that emerged and remained is readily accessible to everyone at any time. In fact, we have all experienced this no-mind awareness repeatedly as a natural aspect of everyday life. However, most likely we did not notice its occurrence or understand it.

Beginning with the awakening in 2002, I experienced an ongoing series of realizations that emerged spontaneously from this direct no-mind awareness about how to live daily life with increased skill, compassion, and joy. These realizations have been clarified and refined in my daily life and my psychotherapy practice over the past 17 years and are immensely useful to anyone seeking to lead a calmer and more joyful life. These realizations which I consider to be gifts from the Holy Spirit, are the core teachings of this book. Awakening happens on its own and is outside our control. However, an accurate understanding of the causes of suffering and the way to be free of it may help prepare the soil for the seed of awakening to take root and flourish.

Some of the best descriptions of the awakening experienced in 2002 have come from spiritual and religious literature based on the personal, profound perceptual shift experienced by the founders of those religions using the language of their time. In this book I will be using ordinary, contemporary language that incorporates a psychological perspective. To that end, it is my hope the ideas I set forth in this book will resonate with you in a deeply personal way. As much as possible I try to utilize ordinary English language to describe and elucidate these experiences and realizations. Occasionally it will be helpful to employ words common to ancient religious traditions. In the Glossary you will find definitions and explanations for a few of the more uncommon terms.

Chapter Two

THE NO-PATH TO AWAKENING

Question: *What then is the Way?*
Answer: *Free of all standards, discriminations,*
                And desires.

Zen Master Nyuri
(Soko Morinaga, 1988, p. 26)

Awake and Alive

If you are sure you want to awaken, take the first step now and drop all your cherished beliefs and concepts. Lose complete interest in everything that's important to you. It is especially important to lose interest in your*self*. Throughout our lives we continually create this imaginary entity known as *me*. We are taught to do this from childhood by well-meaning parents and family. Originally quite enjoyable, this self-creation process eventually proves to be endless, fruitless, boring, tedious, and frustrating. Our attempts to fulfill the ever-changing desires of this fantasized me are not only boring, they are also harmful and destructive and prevent us from enjoying our daily life.

We think we must continue to create ourselves because that's what we have been taught. The notion that we could simply cease this self-creation process is unknown to us. In fact, such an idea may seem crazy. A few years ago, I rode a Greyhound bus from New York City to Binghamton. A college student from Cornell sat directly behind me. Her head and mine were no more than three feet apart. As soon as the bus left the Port Authority, she pulled out her cell phone and began talking in a normal voice with a girlfriend in Ithaca. Unfortunately, I was forced to listen to the conversation that lasted for the entire three-hour trip. I could have asked her to stop talking and put her phone away so that I might enjoy the quiet, but it seemed cruel. It seemed to me as if her survival depended on talking, although from my perspective nothing that was said seemed meaningful or important. I wondered why these two intelligent young women needed to talk about trivia for so long, especially given that probably ten innocent bus passengers in addition to me were forced to involuntarily listen to their conversation. From no-mind awareness the answer came: *they talk to reassure themselves that they are alive.*

The terror of nonbeing controls our every movement. The truth is the cessation of the ordinary notion of who we are leads to incredible freedom and joy. The very experience we fear most is the source of our liberation.

We are programmed to treasure and adore this imaginary, predictable, boring, trivial, self-centered *me*. This self, which we create moment-to-moment, is historic, meaning it occurs in space and time with a beginning and an end. This manufactured self is born and eventually dies. It is both good and bad, knows right from wrong and experiences before and after. This made up self-identity deeply values its endless and meaningless preferences, opinions, feelings and beliefs.

Each individual self is unique. The differences that exist between the self and others are, for the most part, trivial; but our constructed self holds its own differences very dear and magnifies their importance. That which defines us as separate and different from others is also that which permits us to pretend that our individual existence is of extreme importance. We constantly advocate for the needs and wishes of this concocted self. This self has no underlying existence or continuity in time and space. From this perspective, the self is an insubstantial phantom. When we attempt to grasp it, it is gone. It is fleeting, ephemeral. A Zen koan challenges us to *show me your original face before your parents were born.* This koans resolution, when eventually revealed shows our true Self was never born and will never die. Our challenge, then, is to be who we always have been and can't *not* be.

If we stop creating this imaginary self, nothing remains. It is entirely gone, like waking up from a dream. When the body and mind die physically, the historic self dies also. Our physical body and thinking mind are who and what we believe we are. Of course, in one sense we really are this body and mind. However, we are simultaneously so much more, infinitely more. The more part is difficult to describe but can be experienced directly. I mention that we are so much more than we believe we are because it is important to hear this truth even if it makes no sense to you now. Who we are in the absolute sense is not definable or limited by space and time. We are one with and literally the same as the Absolute. We are the mind of Christ as the Apostle Paul says. We are one with and not fundamentally different from the Buddha mind or no-mind awareness. The beautiful phrase *before Abraham was, I AM* (John 8:58) says it so very clearly. We fail to understand Christ's message when we believe that we are separate from or less than all of this. Our normal understanding of who and what we are is profoundly limited by the mistaken beliefs and assumptions about reality we seem to hold so dear.

An example of a mistaken belief is the assumption that who we are is limited to this physical body and the mind that seems to be inside it. We are this, but this is at most only a small part of who and what we are. We have learned to overvalue and needlessly treasure this constructed, historic and limited version of all that we are. Consequently, we worry and fret endlessly over perceived slights and affronts to this tiny and limited version of ourselves. We attempt to guard and protect it, to satisfy its whims, to accept as truth its assumptions, opinions, beliefs, and judgments. Because of this mistaken belief in a very limited version of our infinite true nature, we live in the world feeling vulnerable, fragile and defensive. How would it feel to live in the world without worrying about protecting ourselves? Can you imagine how freeing it would be?

We falsely believe that the imaginary and limited concept of who we are has its own independent existence. It doesn't. The instant we cease creating this fantasy of a *me*, it's gone like a wisp of smoke blown away by a strong wind. The final lines of the *Diamond Sutra* describe clearly our insubstantial nature (Low, 2000, p. 82):

> *Thus, shall you think of all this fleeting world:*
> *A star at dawn, a bubble in a stream;*
> *A flash of lightning in a summer cloud,*
> *A flickering lamp, a phantom and a dream.*

Each image in these lines appears briefly as an object seemingly real and then is gone. Each image is a metaphor for our real nature. A bubble in a stream has a kind of phenomenal reality, but it cannot be grasped. It is insubstantial, fleeting, and ephemeral. So it is with our lives. We have a brief physical existence, and then all that we believe we are ceases. It is no wonder that we have such a monumental fear of death.

Looking deeply inside ourselves, where is the *me*, the one we assume is in charge of our lives? Can you find it? It's as if we assume there is this tiny being right behind our eyes. But is there such a being? Or do we just assume there is? We can find our physical features such as our hands or our nose, but can we find the one that has them? This questioning must be deep, consuming, and persistent for us to realize what is real. Notice the reluctance we can experience to embrace this questioning. We are holding on tightly, but to what? And is what we are holding onto real or imagined? Is there a difference between the two? The deep, consuming and persistent questioning must continue, day and night, thorough sleeping, dreaming and waking states of consciousness. To penetrate to the heart of this matter requires a passionate, consuming and relentless search on our part. We must deeply question the assumptions we were taught as children and have never thought about since.

Encouragement to Seek

In Luke 11, v. 9-10, Jesus teaches his apostles:

> *So I say to you: Ask and it will be given to you; seek and you will find; knock and the door will be opened to you. For everyone who asks receives; the one who seeks finds; and to the one who knocks, the door will be opened.*

This wonderful passage offers tremendous encouragement and reassurance. If we truly seek, we will find. But it is necessary to seek, and it is crucial to understand how to seek. Real seeking involves a profound questioning of all our assumptions and convictions.

We may begin to feel like Alice in Wonderland when she fell down the rabbit hole into a strange new world of Mad Hatters and tea parties as we seriously pursue this path of deconstruction of everything we have assumed to be true. At the very least, a sense of discomfort begins to rise as our automatic moorings loosen. Still, we need to persist.

Who am I?

We often describe ourselves in terms of enduring qualities. For example, I am a short, older white guy who grew up in the South. This description is vaguely accurate with respect to my body, but who is the *I* that inhabits it?

With consistent questioning, examination, and direct experience, the I is realized to be largely a fantasy born of programmed groupthink and mass delusion. This belief system is universal. There is no one to blame for this misunderstanding of reality we have had for our entire life. Our only task is to see clearly what is right in front of our eyes. The miraculous aspect is that dropping our fantasies and living in reality is possible for every one of us. It takes a willingness and desire on our part to move towards the light. Our efforts benefit all beings. Know that you, the reader, have what it takes to do this. Faith in yourself is important. All great spiritual teachers provide encouragement to all of us to simply begin. We begin without knowing exactly how to proceed, where we are going, when or if we will arrive, and what it will be like when we do arrive. The serious pursuit of spiritual freedom is a difficult path. It is literally the hero's journey of myth and fable.

Our true self includes the constructed, historic self-identity. However, we are not only the limited *I* that is born, lives, and dies. We are also infinite, limitless, without form or structure, and beyond space and time. In this aspect, there is no sense of a personal *me*. The self-identity is included in our new and expanded understanding of who we are but is recognized to be incredibly limited. We are much greater than we normally realize. As we identify more and more with the Self, our previously limited self-identity becomes infinitely expanded.

Words and concepts are of little use in this strange, empty world where what we know or think we know gets in the way much more than helps. It's only by becoming one with all that is in the deepest sense that we can freely and spontaneously know this original, limitless, without form or structure, beyond space and time truth of who we are. Once we intimately know the infinite, formless ground of our being, our original Self is free to operate unhindered in our day-to-day life, shining light where before there had been darkness.

Dharma Gates

The third of the four vows taken by Zen Buddhists is the following:

Dharma Gates without number I vow to penetrate...

These gates are the imaginary barriers to awakening that we construct from our false beliefs about reality. We create them and then feel trapped in a fantasy prison of our own making. At the beginning of the spiritual path it seems we are banging hard on the impenetrable walls of our jail cell. I remember sitting in a seven-day Zen meditation retreat called *sesshin*. I had the clear impression of drilling with a diamond drill bit into the infinitely thick cast iron wall of my jail cell. After endless very painful and difficult drilling, I checked my progress, only to find a tiny puff of smoke and no damage to the wall. This is what I had accomplished with my all-out persistent effort. How incredibly frustrating this struggle felt at that time.

In the Zen tradition, after a student's awakening and the successful passing of over 100 introductory koans, the Zen student faces the Mumonkan, a collection of koans compiled in the ninth century by Zen master Mumon. The English translation of Mumonkan is gateless gate or barrier. Mumon had an exquisite sense of humor! There is no gate because there is no barrier. We simply misperceive that we are locked in a jail cell. In fact, there is no cell, nor anyone striving to leave it!

The primary barrier to clearly seeing the truth is our persistent illusion of a continuous presence of some kind that is somewhere inside this human body. We continue this painful and exhaustive effort to define a continuous *me* out of habit, never once asking ourselves what the purpose of defining and believing in a continuous me is. Because it involves the construction of a fantasy, the habitual attempt to create a continuous me is analogous to Sisyphus relentlessly pushing his gigantic boulder uphill only to have it roll back down on him as he nears the top.

The creation of a continuous self-identity takes an immense toll on us and on those with whom we interact. This process of self-creation goes on unabated until we die or until we can no longer continue this fruitless attempt to manufacture a continuous me due to some situation beyond our control, such as a cognitive incapacity like a stroke. Jill Bolte Taylor, PhD, describes the awakening she experienced as a result of a stroke in her video and book *My Stroke of Insight: A Brain Scientist's Personal Journey* (2006). This profound book describes the possibilities that arise when physiological changes in the body prevent the pursuit of our self-creation efforts. Fortunately for us, the destruction of our left frontal lobe, as happened to Dr. Taylor, is not the only way to arrive home.

Awakening is the word we use to describe the experience of ceasing to fabricate the fantasy of a *me*. The deep truth of this is our becoming aware that awakening is a *ceasing,* not a *becoming. The Ceasing of Notions* (Soko Morinaga, 1988) is an obscure Zen Buddhist text written around 600 AD. The title accurately describes the process of awakening. *Notions,* as used here, refers to beliefs, concepts, ideas, and thoughts. A notion is anything the concept-forming, language addicted thinking mind creates. A notion about reality is not reality itself. Ordinarily we mistake the idea for the substance, the shadow for the thing itself. There is a fundamental disconnect between our idea or concept of something and the thing itself. There is only one way to truly know the taste of an orange, and that is to taste the orange ourselves. As Jesus says to the Samaritan woman at the well (John 4:4-26), drink the *living water* and you will thirst no more. If you really want to know what an orange tastes like, you must bite into one yourself. No one can taste it for you.

Once I was sparring with my karate teacher Sensei Hidy Ochiai in class. It was a particularly grueling training experience. At the end he said, *Your cup is so full, I can't pour any tea into it.* This comment is an allusion to the famous Zen story in which a student asks a master to teach him. Without a word, the master begins to pour tea into the student's cup. As the cup overflows, the master continues to pour. Finally, the student exclaims that his cup is overflowing. The master explains to his student that the student's mind is so full that it is not possible for the master to add new understanding. In this same way, Master Ochiai was commenting on my lack of presence as he attempted to teach me during sparring.

As this story makes clear, we must begin a genuine spiritual path by emptying ourselves of all that we think we know. This process is like the first step of Alcoholics Anonymous where the alcoholic must accept that he or she is powerless over alcohol. We too are powerless over our own preferences, beliefs and assumptions. In a similar manner, for us to embrace this new path, we must acknowledge that our efforts up to this point have not led to peace or contentment. We must recognize our own suffering and the suffering of others and open ourselves to a different way of knowing reality.

Zen Buddhists revere Bodhidharma as the Indian Buddhist monk who brought Zen to China. According to traditional wisdom, *If Bodhidharma had a single thought in his head when he came from the west, he would have been useless to everyone.* Bodhidharma was one of the first Buddhist teachers in China to convey the direct way of knowing that occurs outside of words and letters. Our thinking mind can't grasp this form of knowing, yet it is real and profound. The best way to teach and convey this direct way of knowing has been the occupation of Zen teachers ever since the days of Bodhidharma.

In this direct way of knowing, nothing is gained, and all is lost. Therefore, awakening is not a self-improvement project. We do not become a better version of ourselves. In fact, we do not become anything at all. We stop creating fantasies in our head about reality, and we stop behaving as if those fantasies are real. The experience of this *ceasing to become* is freedom. Once the spark ignites in us to pursue this path, the false belief that we are in charge of our life begins to gradually disappear.

How Do You Begin?

A good first step is to gain as accurate an intellectual understanding of this process as possible. If you are a visual learner, I encourage you to read and absorb this and other books that speak to you. Numerous excellent choices are noted for you in this book's bibliography. If you learn best through face-to-face encounters, seek out genuine teachers. If you are an auditory learner, purchasing some CDs or DVDs recorded by genuine teachers would be your best choice. Still others learn best through kinesthetic feedback, such as that provided by formal sitting meditation, yoga, Chi Kung, Tai Chi, or the traditional martial arts. Consult the Resources section in the back of this book for possible options that may appeal to you. Spend a little time in reflection to discern which learning style might work best for you. If one doesn't seem to work well, it is fine to try another. You will ultimately find your best style and will settle comfortably into that learning mode.

Awakening Outside Monastery Walls

Many spiritual seekers throughout the world are deeply immersed in this radical deconstruction process on their own with little structure, support or connection with any traditional spiritual discipline that is focused on becoming aware of our true nature, such as Zen, Vipassana and Tibetan Buddhism or Advaita Vedanta. Yet, doing so has some significant drawbacks. Taking this journey alone cannot offer a supportive community of like-minded seekers or a disciplined practice, both of which can make the required deconstruction of the historic *me* less traumatic and destabilizing. In addition, going it alone means missing out on the quality control and informed critical evaluation regarding student claims of awakening that can be provided by a deeply realized teacher (see *Halfway up the Mountain: The Error of Premature Claims of Enlightenment*, by Mariana Caplan, 1999). From my perspective, the most significant drawback to taking this journey on your own could be the absence of an awakened teacher to guide the seeker on their path.

Having personal access to an awakened teacher who manifests direct realization in their everyday behavior is extremely valuable. In the past, such individuals were rare and often were secluded in monastic settings or were otherwise unknown or inaccessible to ordinary people. Today it is possible to access YouTube and, using some skillful discernment, find a variety of awakened teachers manifesting direct realization in their own unique manner. While this presents the seeker with a wonderful opportunity, familiarity can create a false sense of understanding. It's one thing to grasp intellectually the theory and philosophy of self-realization. It's entirely different to see directly for yourself. By reading contemporary authors, listening to audio recordings of awakened teachers giving spiritual talks, and watching videos, it is possible to grasp the message in an intellectual manner. However, accurate intellectual understanding can take us only so far. An awakened teacher, on the other hand, will recognize how far along the path to direct realization the student has travelled, and can guide the student to further deconstruct his or her self-identification.

For this reason, the most advantageous portal to direct realization is to spend as much time as possible in the physical presence of a living awakened teacher. In the presence of such a teacher, the obsessing mind becomes quiet. Shakyamuni Buddha describes it as a transmission from mind to mind. A contemporary example of this process would be Ramesh Balsekar (1999). Balsekar was a successful,

Westernized Indian banker fluent in English. After his retirement from banking, he became a translator for Nisargadatta Maharaj in his frequent interactions with English-speaking spiritual seekers. Apparently, after only two or three years of interaction with Marahaj as his translator, Balsekar experienced an awakening. We can assume Ramesh brought to his interaction with Nisargadatta a profound openness and need to know directly for himself.

An awakened teacher can provide invaluable help in avoiding pitfalls and detours on the spiritual path. By continually bringing our attention to what is essential, a teacher reminds us of our true nature. By simply being, the teacher demonstrates the way home for us. It's as if the teacher is repeatedly saying and manifesting, *This is it; this is how it is. Just this; right here, right now. Look and see.* The energetic presence of a teacher provides a direct portal to realization for the student. Being in the physical presence of an awakened teacher is usually far more powerful than experiencing the teachings of an awakened teacher through books, video or audio.

An effective student-teacher relationship requires direct engagement, transparency, and openness. The teacher can point out blind spots in a student's practice or unevenness in the student's direct realization. Additionally, the teacher can point out glimpses of direct awareness the student is experiencing but has not recognized. The teacher can provide accurate intellectual understanding when the student has experienced a certain measure of direct realization, thus further deepening the student's awareness. The teacher facilitates and fine tunes the birth process of the student's alchemical transformation of consciousness resulting from the spontaneous emergence of direct realization.

One significant problem for many aspiring spiritual seekers is the belief that they can recognize someone who is an awakened teacher without having experienced at least a glimpse of their own awakening.

Our ego convinces us that we can make accurate assessments by observing certain behaviors and personal qualities of the teacher. In fact, truly enlightened people are rare and have no distinguishing characteristics. Albert Low observes, *An awakened person can't be recognized by any outward sign or manifestation, even after that person has undergone years of patient, gradual practice after awakening* (Low, p. 47).

A genuine awakening does not conform to our beliefs about how it should look. Nisargadatta Maharaj, one of the greatest awakened teachers of the 20th century, sold and enjoyed smoking cigarettes and other tobacco products. I was told I could not have awakened because at the time I was neither celibate nor vegetarian. I myself once believed I could never wake up deeply since I was not a monastic. I would learn that such ideas are ridiculous. In fact, all ideas about how an awakened being looks or acts are necessarily false because awakening does not obey any rules or regulations.

Respect Individual Affinities

It's important for us to always accept and respect individual affinity. For this reason, it can be beneficial to experience different paths and teachers. If we are led to do so, we may choose to experience and experiment with a variety of methods and teachers. Have faith that you will find what works best for you. With a sincere commitment to experiencing your own awakening, which will serve to benefit all beings, you will find your way. Trust in yourself and the light that already exists within you.

Conversely, there can also be some significant advantages to the separation of direct awareness from formal structure or teachings of any kind. Some examples include religions, lineages of teachers, approved scripture, etc. Barry Long, Eckhart Tolle, Byron Katie and many others have provided a wonderful service in helping to liberate direct awareness from traditional disciplines, many of which can sometimes prove to be cultish, elitist, misogynist, secretive, incomprehensible and obscure.

Awareness cannot be contained nor defined by anything. In direct realization, everything that has been learned needs to be unlearned. All that is known must become unknown. Jesus says in the Gospel of Luke (13:30), *the first will be last and the last will be first.* Like so many sayings of Jesus, this comment has multiple levels of meaning. As applied to awakening, it says to me what I have observed, namely, that worldly success does not necessarily correlate highly with spiritual aptitude.

Direct, immediate, experiential awakening is available to all. It's no longer possible or, for that matter, desirable to isolate and restrict the pursuit of realization to monastic communities or ashrams. How then do we proceed?

Portals to Awakening

There are three major and time-honored paths to awakening. These portals aren't separate and distinct. Each one overlaps the others. For the sake of discussion, think of these three portals as the doorways of the body, the mind, and the heart. We'll discuss them separately for purposes of illustration. There aren't three paths or portals; there isn't even one. Huang Po puts it succinctly, *When body and mind achieve spontaneity, The Way is reached and Mind is understood.* (Blofeld, 1958, p. 55).

Path of the Body

We gain enormous benefits in activities that challenge our less developed strengths and talents. I experienced this firsthand when around the age of forty, I decided to learn karate. I had by then a long-standing interest in Zen Buddhism. I checked out two local martial arts schools that were highly regarded. One school taught the Korean martial art *Tae Kwon Do*. The other school taught a Japanese style of karate called *Washin Ryu*. Both seemed well-run and organized, but I chose to pursue *Washin Ryu* because of the teacher. Sensei Hidy Ochiai, who grew up in a Zen Buddhist temple in Japan, was the head of this school and became my teacher. Sensei Ochiai's profound understanding of the way of no-mind in action heavily influenced his teaching. I continued regular training for fifteen years and developed many abilities that were heretofore unknown to me. I am grateful to Sensei Ochiai for his profound teaching.

Possibly the greatest benefit of disciplined training in martial arts for the serious spiritual student comes from the requirement to pay close attention to the body. It's impossible to do any martial art, yoga, or other body-oriented disciplines while at the same time persisting in an obsessive preoccupation with our own thoughts. The *no-mind* approach of total absorption in the present moment is required to perform any sport or mind-body discipline at a high level. In Western terms, the total absorption that leads to the disappearance of self-awareness could be called being in the zone or *flow* (Csikszentmihalyi, M., 2008).

Many years ago, I experienced this flow during the last five minutes of a 5K race. The experience was purely delightful, effortless running. I had no sense of my feet hitting the pavement. I felt timeless, perfect, and wonderful with no awareness of fatigue or muscle soreness, and ultimately ran the fastest 5K of my life, lopping a full minute off my previous best time.

Flow is more likely when the thinking mind is completely quiet, although a quiet external environment is not required. Many of us have experienced these blissful moments of no-mind presence. It's valuable to notice and remember these experiences when they happen.

To do so seems to increase the likelihood of experiencing them again. Experiencing these blissful moments gives us our own personal taste of our own unconditioned awareness.

Once in karate class I was sparring with my teacher Sensei Ochiai. Connecting with a punch or a kick was not the purpose of the exercise. Sensei's purpose was to teach through demonstration what the student needed to learn, without any preconceived ideas and without verbal statements.

As I began to spar with Sensei, I felt myself shift into a timeless dimension. This experience, as with all glimpses of pure awareness, happened in a completely unpremeditated, unexpected manner. The experience was of sparring happening on its own with no one doing it. It was effortless, more like an exquisite dance of oneness. Sensei and I were not two. Yet we were not the same either. While the words I use to describe the experience are conceptual, during the experience itself no conceptual thought occurred.

Try not to fall victim to the occasional benefit that comes from obsessional thinking. Allow yourself to learn simply through your physical presence in the world, and in so doing your own intuitive mind will be the path that leads you to the kingdom of heaven on earth.

Path of the Mind

> *So you students of the Way should immediately*
> *Refrain from conceptual thought.*
> *Let a tacit understanding be all.*
> *Any mental process must lead to error.*
>
> Huang Po (Blofeld, J., 1958, p. 42)

It is interesting to me to notice how relentlessly ancient Zen masters cautioned against the use of the thinking mind we generally worship.

Huang Po died in 850 AD. If a general overreliance on the thinking mind was a problem then, I wonder what Huang Po would say now. The way of intellectual understanding is naturally appealing to those who have developed their intellect and found thinking to be satisfying and rewarding. The appeal of thought was and still is enormous for me. Yet, we must recognize that we will never be able to approach awakening through the gate of the intellect if we rely solely on our thinking mind

Thinking is useful when it's actually *thinking*. However, everything we consider thinking is not actual thinking, but rather obsessing, worrying, ruminating, fantasizing, judging others and ourselves, and creating imaginary versions of the past and future. Real thinking, when it's truly needed and beneficial, arises spontaneously on its own. It is productive, solves problems and creates solutions. Ruminating and obsessing is tiring, depleting and without value. We can become mindlessly addicted to thinking as the only or best way to solve problems. Thinking about, describing, and naming life separates us from it. Conceptual thought removes us from the direct experience of what is. Awakening is to know directly without the intervening process of labeling our experience in words.

During a brief lunch break on a perfect summer day approximately thirty-five years ago, I was sitting in the garden of the Rochester Zen Center. After sipping warm miso soup, I looked up and directly in front of me, approximately fifteen yards away, I saw a small, Japanese Red Oak tree. My experience of seeing it was indescribable. I was fully present to what was right in front of my eyes. At that time, I had no words to communicate my experience. Now, I can explain that this was possibly the first time that I consciously saw what was in front of me without labeling, commenting on, judging, appreciating, or evaluating. I saw the oak tree *itself* without the intervening use of language that would have served no useful purpose, but rather would have deadened the direct experience of what was actually *so*.

When the mind is quiet, an awareness of all sense impressions arises spontaneously, and no words are needed or desired. If we are addicted to and identify with the thinking mind, we cannot be fully present in our life. Instead, we live a pale imitation of life constructed by our verbal concepts, assumptions, beliefs and opinions.

To release our addiction to thinking, we need to use the thought process itself to deconstruct the belief systems that control and limit us. While it's impossible to deliberately stop thinking, what does work is to observe the content of our mind with curiosity and acceptance. With enough dispassionate observation, we eventually lose interest in our own thoughts. This loss of interest happens because the content of our mind is boring, repetitive and tedious. It seems we must observe our mind to become free of it. With enough self-observation, we'll naturally conclude for ourselves that the normal content of our minds is without value. For many of us, such a thought can bring up an intense fear that if we believe our thoughts are without value, we will disappear. The truth is, there is nothing to fear, because we do not disappear. We do not cease. Awareness continues. To accept that the normal content of our minds is without value liberates us. It does not destroy us. This, then, is the nature of spiritual awakening.

This dramatic ceasing of needless mental activity is certainly how it was for me. Although each person's experience is unique, I believe this cessation of needless mental activity is very common with a deep and abiding awakening. The mind becomes much quieter, with thoughts arising only when needed and beneficial. The chatter in our minds sharply diminishes. Real thinking that is productive and useful increases, while the fake thinking that is obsessing, ruminating, and worrying largely ceases.

Simultaneously, actively fantasizing about imaginary past and future events no longer occurs. Virtually everything we think about the past and the future is a fantasy. Memories are fantasies because they are being actively created in the moment of remembering. The future has not happened yet, so it doesn't exist. All we can know about the future is a fantasy we create in the present. With the spontaneous cessation of all this needless mental activity, the mind becomes calmer and quieter.

An extremely nervous person will find sitting still to be difficult, almost impossible. Every time they try to be still, they quickly notice that they're tapping their feet, wriggling in their chair, scratching their head, coughing, grimacing, stretching, and yawning. However, with the cessation of needless mental activity, they find that suddenly their anxiety disappears. Their body naturally grows still because there's no need for useless movement. They are not nearly as tired at the end of the day because they have not been taxing their mind or constantly moving their body all day. Their body is relaxed in the evening instead of tight and agitated. Life becomes a pleasure instead of a chore. They are no longer fighting their way through life. Instead, they are relaxed, able to let go and fully enjoy the experiences life brings. It is as if they have been born again, and they have.

Path of the Heart

The path of the heart would be the natural path for people who value being able to feel their emotions. In this path, we allow our heart to melt. Oneness with the felt experience of others comes naturally. However, we can impede the progress of this by trying to analyze, control or name our experience. With the growth and expansion of our awareness, we become more open to respond freely, directly, and spontaneously to whatever is in front of us.

People who do not easily recognize their inner felt sense (Gendlin, 1998) will find attending to the inner experience of feelings and sensations in the body helpful in becoming more open, accepting and expressive. Radical acceptance of our own inner experience facilitates our ability to feel and demonstrate more loving kindness and compassion to our self and others.

Naming Our Experience

> *The source of heaven and earth is without form or substance*
> *Naming creates the ten thousand things.*
>
> Tao Te Ching
> (Marshall, B., 2009, p. 155)

People often struggle to accurately identify and name their emotions. They may believe if they can find a name for the emotion they are having, they can control it. The best approach to powerful emotions is to remain open and present to the emotion; to sit with and experience any reactions that arise because of the emotion. If we allow our emotions to just be, without adding or subtracting anything, we liberate ourselves from our struggle to name our feelings. It's important to note that as we sit quietly with our emotions, it is possible that words will occur to us that accurately describe the experience we are having. This naturally occurring naming of our experience is often quite helpful in reducing emotional discomfort. Whatever we feel is ok, just as it is. We just need to simply notice our inner experience. Whatever comes up for us, we need to allow it to be, exactly as it is.

As our identification with the self-absorbed ego begins to disappear, the buffers that protect us from direct experience begin to dissolve. Spontaneous feelings will arise. We might find ourselves feeling deeply touched by an experience that previously would not have affected us. The thinking mind, which is still active, may want to question and judge such feelings and experiences. We might feel tempted to argue with ourselves over whether our emotional response to an experience is appropriate. As much as possible, we need to try to quiet the mental chatter and simply allow ourselves to accept whatever emotion we are experiencing. We need to welcome this opportunity to connect more to what is real for us. This is radical self-acceptance. Because most of us are highly skilled at suppressing or denying our inner experience, we need to be patient with ourselves as we learn this new skill of accurate, honest self-awareness. How we express a feeling can be appropriate or inappropriate, but the feeling itself is neither right nor wrong. Feelings simply *are*.

Devotional Practice

The heart path is often associated with more devotional spiritual practices as found in all major religious traditions. We need to follow our heart in determining which spiritual practices resonate with us. These practices can include rituals, prayers, service work for the benefit of others, chanting, and prostrations to name just a few. All devotional practices can remind us of what is most real in our daily life. They can also help us lose interest in our own constructed self as we let the light of love and wisdom permeate us. In the Gospel of Luke, Jesus says, *Yet not my will, but yours be done.* (Luke 22:42). Our goal is to continually surrender our self to the will of God.

We need to trust our heart when it comes to devotional practices. We need to notice how we feel during and after such practices. We need to continue to do what helps us to soften and open. Vulnerability is natural. We need to welcome vulnerability as a sign of a shift in consciousness.

By engaging in devotional practices, we weaken our attachment to obsessive thinking, worry, and self-preoccupation. Devotional practices assist us in becoming more aware and present in the world. While reading about spiritual practices has value, consciously engaging in a practice allows us to experience it for ourselves and is infinitely more powerful.

My own path has been largely a devotional one. I read very little scripture or other writings on spiritual truth before I experienced my own shift in consciousness in 2002. Yet, when this awakening to no-mind awareness arose in me, a passionate need to know more about how others describe and communicate their new understanding occurred. Consequently, for the first time I began to deeply immerse myself in reading about the awakening experiences of others. I also sharply increased my practice of Zen Buddhism, which emphasizes self-reliance and individual effort supported by proper guidance and counsel. I also benefitted from participation in a community of serious practitioners who actively pursued the path of awakening.

Know for Yourself

This direct seeing is available to everyone. No one can give it to us, and no one can withhold it from us. We can know the word of God directly for ourselves. We are all born in the image of God, one with the creator of heaven and earth. If we feel distant from God, it is because our thinking mind has caused us to turn away from what is directly revealed. When we experience direct awareness, we then know the truth that God is, has always been and will always be as close to us as our breath.

Chapter Three

A MIND IS A TERRIBLE PLACE TO BE

If you never had another thought in your head for the rest of your life, who would be reading this?

We define ourselves in a variety of ways. How should we describe ourselves to someone we don't know? What should we include? What should we leave out? We all write this self-description in our minds every day. It is one way we reinvent ourselves and bring ourselves into being moment to moment. We continue this process of self-invention our entire life. What if we let it drop completely, right now?

As we progress through this adventure of becoming more awake and present, we also become more accepting of ourselves just as we are. We are far less interested in comparing ourselves to others or to some imaginary ideal in our head of what we should be like. We learn to treasure who we are right now without apology or a need to explain or justify. Genuine self-respect and self-acceptance are very different from narcissism and ego cherishing.

The Red Ferrari: Fantasy vs. Reality

I have had a love affair with cars since I was a teenager. A favorite car fantasy I had was to one day own a bright red Ferrari. My fantasy was realized in part many years ago when one afternoon I had the good fortune to drive a Ferrari. Bob, the owner of the Ferrari, was a friend of a friend. He had just purchased a red Ferrari and I was able to visit

Bob to see it. The car was a 1982 Mondial coupe and it was gorgeous. I felt blessed to be in its presence. To my utter astonishment and great joy, Bob offered to let me drive his new toy, and with great delight I accepted. Bob not only let me drive it, he also let me drive it fast and for as long as I wanted.

Driving the car, I quickly became aware of the downsides to owning a Ferrari. For example, every time I stopped at a red light, a teenage boy would pull up next to me, gun his engine, and apparently want to race. I began to see how this could get old fast. Additionally, parking the car was nerve-wracking as I felt anxious about the possibility of it being damaged. Even just filling the gas tank was another adventure, both in expense and in conversation. I felt obliged to discuss the car with virtually every male that saw it because they all wanted to talk with me about it. I also dealt with being followed by curiosity seekers who just wanted to get a closer look. Moreover, the process for changing the oil in a Ferrari is a complex one indeed. It required a multi-day trip to a Ferrari dealer at a cost of approximately $1,500.00, absent the need for parts or any other repair. I could feel the dream I had to own a Ferrari begin to fade. At one point, my younger son bought me a brilliant red Ferrari cap at a Ferrari showroom on a trip he took to Italy. Ownership of this cap is now as close as I ever want to get to owning a real Ferrari.

SUGGESTED PRACTICE

Remember times in your life when you got something that was very important to you. Ideally, what you received would be something you desperately wanted. For example, it could be a romantic relationship, or a job offer for which you had worked so hard. Did getting what you want give you lasting peace and contentment? It's possible to satisfy ego-based cravings momentarily. What usually follows satisfying a craving though, is a let-down. Once we've satisfied the craving, we

> *find ourselves on a quest to find something else to satisfy us. Typically, this seeking and questing continues until we die.*
>
> *Take some time now to reflect on your genuine accomplishments in getting what you wanted. How did you feel? How long did it last? What happened next?*

With some self-reflection, it becomes obvious that our lives primarily consist of dashed dreams and frustrated wishes. We are not, seemingly by nature, satisfied with things as they are in the present moment. It is the nature of the conditioned mind to continually seek.

This constant seeking and searching for more, or different, or better, or less, keeps us locked in a vicious cycle. In awakening, we learn the fundamental truth that to let go of all that we think we are will not destroy us. It will liberate us.

The great injunction given to us by Jesus Christ and other awakened teachers is to experience a spiritual death and rebirth. Once we experience this, the thought of the eventual physical death of our body is of little consequence. We become aware of the fact that the ground of our true being is eternal.

As in my story of the red Ferrari, we all eventually learn that no matter how important something seems, once we have it, we will lose a lot of our original interest in it and begin a new quest for something else. The only exception to this rule is the quest for awakening. When you experience it directly, there is no more seeking for more or better or different. We realize that there is nothing but *this*, just as it is, now and forever.

Awakening? Say *What?*

Awakening refers to a direct, personal realization that the belief in an inner, organizing principle called *me* is illusory. In this direct experiential realization, you come to know that the you that had always seemed so important does not exist. You find it possible to do everything you currently do and to know everything you currently know without adding the superfluous concept of me.

In this experience, there is a direct experiential realization of the absence of an enduring, consistent personal identity. This realization is so obvious and self-evident that once we realize it, we cannot fathom how we missed it during all those years of seeking.

We use the word *belief* to describe what we do not *know*. In the ordinary relative world, it is not a belief that we have two hands; it is a fact. It is not a belief that our eyes are horizontal and our nose vertical. It is the truth. In awakening, we do not *believe*. We *know*. We know reality as it is instead of how we believe it should be. Moreover, we ultimately experience the nearly complete dissolution of our identification with the programmed, conditioned entity we call *me,* or *I*. David Godman addresses this process in detail in his three-volume biography of Papaji *Nothing Ever Happened* (1998).

We live in an age when we can go on the Internet and easily order books, DVDs, and streaming video by many wise teachers of true nondual wisdom who offer their insights in relatively clear and helpful terms. During the past fifty years, there has been a literal explosion of both original and translated literature describing nearly all aspects of the awakening process. Yet there is both an upside and downside to such easy accessibility.

Intellectual Understanding is not Enough

The upside is that previously difficult to access teachings are readily available courtesy of the internet. More people than ever now can access high-level teaching. On the surface, this vast and rapid increase in accessibility benefits everyone on the planet. However, the downside is that these difficult teachings are available so easily. This easy accessibility can breed a false sense of mastery. Many people have an excellent intellectual understanding of the concepts involved in enlightenment, awakening and nondual literature. Yet, without a direct, personal experiential realization the seeker merely has an intellectual understanding. The two are not the same and to only have an intellectual understanding is not the experience of awakening itself.

I have read voraciously throughout most of my life, but my conceptual understanding of the awakening process occurred only *after* experiential knowing had emerged on its own. Reading high-level spiritual truth prior to awakening may be beneficial, but only to a limited extent. The primary purpose of such reading is to encourage spiritual practice and persistent effort. In traditional Zen teaching, experiential knowing is the benchmark. This truth makes itself known to you at the right time on the journey to awakening.

Developing the Intent to Awaken

Most initial awakenings are brief glimpses that have a beginning and an end. However brief and transitory the initial glimpse of *no-mind* may be, the experience is profound and transformative. Even a brief glimpse of direct, unconditioned awareness turns ordinary life upside down and inside out.

Glimpses of awakening allow us to dwell in reality as it is, not as we wish it were or believe it should be. Once we have experienced some degree of this, even briefly, we can never again be satisfied with the world of illusion. Our goals and priorities shift. Our primary goal becomes experiencing the ongoing awareness of the presence of God in all things. Living directly in this awareness, we realize all our previously held ego-driven beliefs were untrue.

Nothing mystical or otherworldly surrounds this process. We accept, embrace, and become one with what already is. *This* is the true miracle. We learn to live in reality as it is, valuing and appreciating everything exactly as it is, needing nothing to be different. Awakening to reality is the end of seeking and striving. We realize that everything, including our self is simply the way it is, nothing more, nothing less. We begin to surrender our ego-driven beliefs and in that process, we experience true spiritual awakening.

In a subtle yet infinitely powerful manner, the source of all that is guides everything. This source is not born and does not die. The experiential recognition that you are now, always have been, and always will be one with this source is the beginning of the awakening journey. When you become aware of this, you will automatically notice the free action of the source of all that is in the world. *This* is who and what you truly are.

If we pay close attention to our inner experience, and not just to our thoughts and beliefs, we will often notice a profound sense of estrangement and alienation. This deep feeling of loss of identity, this yearning to return to our true home, drives us towards spiritual practice. This is an important step towards realizing that we never left our true home, so we don't need to return. What we seek is already ours as our birthright. Our true nature can neither be lost nor found, just as we cannot lose the sky or the clouds. What we are seeking is already ours.

The most direct way to accomplish this realization for most cerebral Westerners is to observe the content of the mind. The purpose of this self-observation is to facilitate the loss of interest in our ordinary mind, which is full of worry, rumination, greed, self-absorption and preoccupation. When observed objectively, the I we have assumed ourselves to be will be recognized as nothing more than a largely fictional character whose singular goal is gratifying its desires and appeasing its multitude of fears.

Before our awakening, whether we realize it or not, we are essentially a programmed automaton. We persist in the false belief that our programming is our identity. This belief does not serve us well, and if we cling to it, we will be discontented and forever searching for release. One way out of this inherently frustrating and hopeless search for more and better is to observe the content of our mind as often as possible. A related method that will work better for some is to deliberately switch the focus of our observation from our thoughts to the physical sensations in our body, such as the rising and falling of the breath. It can also be helpful to direct our attention outward, focusing intently on the sights, sounds and smells of the natural world. When deeply absorbed with our own suffering it is especially helpful to focus on the experience of others and attempt to assist them in the best way possible. Service to others is a time-honored spiritual path.

We cling to the belief that our thoughts, opinions, and beliefs, all of which we cherish, are true and important. True spiritual growth is the challenging and humbling process of admitting to ourselves that who and what we think we are is a culturally created construct. The genuine path is to become less and less, not more and better.

Does Awakening Produce Sainthood?

Nothing is wrong with becoming a nicer, less angry, and more forgiving person. These are admirable qualities to cultivate. Life will go more smoothly if you gradually become a better citizen, spouse, parent, friend, or employee. When we cultivate compassion and a nonjudgmental attitude towards self and others, we do help make the world a better place in a meaningful way. These are worthy goals, but they have no direct relationship to awakening. Awakening is not the same as becoming a better, kinder, more forgiving person. Rather, awakening is the profound and permanent loss of interest in maintaining the false sense of who we are. With deep awakening, there is no interest in becoming *anything at all*. It is the cessation of our great self-improvement project. The tedium of constantly striving to improve the imaginary self disappears almost completely, returning only rarely, and then often for purposes of amusement.

Path of Direct Awareness

The path of direct awareness is not about fulfilling or depriving the historical self of its desires. Growth does not require deprivation of ordinary human needs for comfort, such as the enjoyment of sensual pleasures including food, sleep, rest, play, companionship, sex, affection, or emotional nurturance. It does, however, require a willingness to question deeply and relinquish everything that up to this point we have believed to be necessary, real and important.

Total immersion is required for this deep questioning to bear fruit. We are not completely in charge of the decision to question everything we believe. Somehow, the awakening path chooses us. Consider this passage from The New Testament:

> *For [God] says to Moses, / I will have mercy on whom/ I have mercy, / and I will have compassion/ on whom I have/ compassion.*
> Romans 9:15–16

Looking back through the lens of awareness, we recognize our deepest wounds and most bitter resentments to be a form of grace. Pain and suffering appear to be the prime motivations to begin serious work on developing clear understanding and awareness. Therefore, our suffering is our greatest gift. Everything that has occurred in our lives, even the most traumatic events that have no imaginable redeeming value, happened for a reason and can be used as motivation for spiritual practice.

From the big-picture perspective, anything that has deeply wounded us or has brought us to our knees is a blessing if it motivates us to do the hard work of becoming consciously aware of our deeply held, automatic assumptions about life. Examined realistically and objectively through the eyes of pure awareness, the assumptions we heretofore cherished are frequently revealed to be at variance with what is true. Seeing everything accurately, as it is, is the way to peace and happiness. Our best interest lies in learning how to recognize reality and live in accordance with it.

As we lose interest in our socially constructed belief systems, it becomes progressively harder for us to accept simple black and white answers that do not align with our own experience. Therefore, our purpose is to search for what is true. Guidance and encouragement from one who has gone through this self-deconstruction process is invaluable, though hard to find. While an experienced guide can point us towards the truth, they will not be able to describe the process with complete accuracy. They can only describe *their* experience of the process, not *ours*.

It is necessary for us to do this work for ourselves. We need to make a serious effort to practice self-observation and find out, through our own experience, if these ideas are true for us. Only then will we notice a real difference in the quality of presence that we bring to our day-to-day life. We cannot get *it* from anywhere. We can only get it from ourselves. We must have faith and courage to take that first step, to summon the commitment to awaken. We need to make perseverance in the pursuit of truth our devotional practice.

Living Words, Dead Words

Virtually everything we normally write or talk about is about something or someone. In writing or talking *about*, there's an inherent separation between the subject and us. This separation is so ubiquitous that we rarely notice it. This kind of writing uses dead words. Dead words are devoid of fire and passion.

Living words convey texture, taste, feel, and smell. Living words put us smack in the middle of the action. Living words don't just describe reality; they demonstrate it. Living words *are* reality. Living words are one with the source; they are spontaneous, unpremeditated, unpredictable, and powerful. Living words have the potential to rattle our cage, to move us away from our comfort zone.

Basho (1644–1694) wrote perhaps the most admired poem in all Japanese literature, quoted here in Robert Aitken's translation *Zen Wave: Basho's Haiku and Zen* (2003, p. 3). It is an extraordinary example of live words:

> *The old pond;*
> *A frog jumps in*
> *The sound of water.*

No dead words here. Each word is vibrant and shimmering.

SUGGESTED PRACTICE

Sit silently now by the same pond as Basho. That pond is right here, right now. Did the frog carefully consider his options before he leapt into vast space? Did he wonder what would happen if his inspired flight went haywire? Is this a demonstration of perfect freedom in action? What would you need to do to become as present as this frog?

> *Close your eyes and visualize yourself sitting by this pond, totally absorbed in the surroundings. Mosquitoes humming, pungent smell of fresh earth, wet air, night falling. Complete stillness, and suddenly out of nowhere an action so direct and free that it is no action.*
>
> *Reflect on the following: Can we be as present as this frog in our daily actions? Can we leap into pure awareness at this moment? Furthermore, who took the leap? Was it the frog or was it Basho? My addendum to Basho's poem:*
>
>> *Old man Basho slogs home, dripping wet,*
>> *Wide-awake;*
>> *Cool night air, crickets chirping,*
>> *Starlight.*

Basho describes this process of being fully awake and alive in ordinary life in another haiku. In this haiku, no one is going anywhere. Yet, movement happens. Leaves swirl in the early autumn mist; darkness falls; silence is everywhere. In this silent walking of no one going anywhere, moving without movement, we find the Source of the mystery Form and emptiness, you and I, before and after, Heaven and Hell: all judgment and discrimination are no more.

> *No one*
> *Walks along this path*
> *This autumn evening.*

(Low, 2006, p. 57)

When Jesus says, *Follow me* (Luke 9:59), he is offering an invitation to take a leap of faith. The man he was speaking with in this passage declines the invitation saying that his father died that day and must be buried before sunset. This was a devout man who carefully observed the rules and regulations of his religion. Jesus' response is powerful, direct, and to the point: *Let the dead bury their own dead, but you go and proclaim the kingdom of God* (Luke 9:60). Jesus' words were alive! There is no fear based slavish devotion to following dead rules here. Jesus recognized the potential for spiritual growth in this man and issued the invitation, but the man himself had to be willing to follow, no matter how alive Jesus' words were.

So, too, it is with us. No matter how clear and direct the invitation, we must be willing to take the leap. It is necessary to die to all we currently believe is real and important, all we think we are. For each person it is a leap into the unknown and requires a heroic effort. We must drop now and forever everything that we currently believe to be true. This death to self is absolute. Yet, this profound invitation is available to all. Basho and Jesus are instructing us. *Be still and know that I am God* (Psalm 46:10).

Seeing with Eyes Wide Open

The same awareness that Jesus manifests in the world is available to us now. It is always everywhere equally. The Self does not vary. It neither increases nor decreases, never more here than there. We can find it everywhere we look if we have eyes to see.

> *Outside my window walk*
> *Father Mother Goose stand guard*
> *Go nowhere goslings.*

This haiku emerged as I was looking out my back window watching two adult geese, presumably a mother and a father, stand sentry over nine baby geese. The parents stood still, facing the river, one looking upstream and the other downstream. The goslings blithely meandered, each in its own world, enjoying the moment and learning to forage for food.

As a parent, I could vividly identify with the alert attention of the adults. Geese must guard their young from danger with hawk-like vigilance. What a rare gift was unfolding in front of my eyes! It was the rare gift of presence made manifest in this world by a pair of geese. The goslings, unstructured, unformed, undisciplined, were freely experiencing the world without thought or fear, and as such were one with all that is.

> *I tell you the truth, unless you change and become like little children, you will never enter the kingdom of heaven.*
> Matthew 1:3

The miracle of awareness is the complete merger, the total oneness of form and emptiness. As awakened adults who are present in this world as it is, we have the natural ability to be vigilantly attentive, just as the parents of the goslings, when we *need* to be vigilant. Yet, equally available to us is the gift of being able to be playfully exuberant, just like the goslings. We can enjoy the gift of being completely absorbed in the present moment only.

We need to always recognize and value living words. We need to be vigilant when we are speaking to others and vigilant in listening to others when they speak. We need to pay special attention to those moments when someone speaks from the heart and notice our feelings in body and mind.

It is our birthright to speak truth. If we speak directly from our heart, our words have wisdom, power, and grace. We all are fully capable of speaking our truth. Personal experience will always show us what is true; all we need to do is surrender. We need to seek out people who use living words, and teachers that nurture aliveness in us. Then, as we grow spiritually, we will move further away from teachings that create fear and constriction.

Arouse the Mind that Seeks the Way

The power of collective conditioning is enormous. How do we generate enough passion and intensity to break free from the mass delusion of separation we believe from birth and that follows us throughout our life? The illusion is that we can find contentment and happiness by satisfying the cravings of the ego. Look at your own life and ask: Has this worked for you? Graced with clear seeing, we can know immediately that who we are is quite different from who we have believed we have been.

How Do You Feel Right Now?

Becoming consciously aware of our inner experience during ordinary activities can be invaluable for reducing chronic levels of tension and anxiety.

SUGGESTED PRACTICE

Observe your inner experience for a few minutes. Don't interfere with the ongoing flow of sensations, feelings and thoughts. Notice the breath. Is it regular, deep and relaxed? Usually the answer will be No.

Without realizing it, we tense the musculature of our body as if bracing for an assault which never arrives. Scan through your body and notice how you feel. Try to maintain a completely permissive and accepting approach.

There is no correct way to feel. Do not attempt to suppress or deny any aspect of your experience. Your goal is simply to be aware, curious and open to your own experience.

Observe the Mind

If we objectively and dispassionately observe the content of our mind or the sensations in our body for a few minutes several times each day, we will be embarking on a remarkable journey toward seeing reality as it is. Many of us think that spiritual practice is about reading, thinking, and understanding spiritual literature. Believing that reading, thinking and understanding spiritual literature is a spiritual practice in and of itself reinforces the mistaken notion that we can use our thinking mind to transcend itself. Nothing could be further from the truth.

We need to observe our thinking mind objectively, and in doing so, we will inevitably lose all interest in it. *This* is the way. In *The Zen Teaching of Huang Po,* the great Chinese Zen master says, *If you can only rid yourselves of conceptual thought, you will have accomplished everything.* (Blofeld, J., 1958, p. 33). Doing so is the first step into the stream of spiritual wisdom.

The flow of mindless chatter is not itself a problem. Our unfortunate identification with the trivial and largely meaningless content of our minds causes the problems we experience. With enough practice, we notice that we take this empty mental chatter much too seriously. When we do so, we experience feelings and sensations and assume that they are important. As we bring our observing awareness to our inner experience, we see over time how we create our own experience by the way we think, interpret, and perceive. To become aware of this process we engage in with our mind is the beginning of freedom.

An important part of this process is to face our own mortality. In the eternal scheme of things, this mortal life is brief. A Zen saying tells us that we must focus and concentrate as if our hair were on fire. Or, said another way, we must develop such a passion to awaken that we seek it with the same intensity that a drowning man seeks to breathe.

Effort is Required

Some current spiritual teachers claim that there's no need to do anything to awaken, that you're already awake, and that you should relax and simply enjoy yourself. While true at the absolute level, these notions, taken literally, will only serve to derail spiritual passion and intent. Jesus enjoins us, *You shall love the Lord your God with all your heart and with all your soul and with all your mind.* (Matthew 22:37–40). Jesus doesn't say, *Don't worry, be happy!* To love the Lord your God with all your heart, soul and mind is a difficult task, indeed.

Albert Low says in *Hakuin on Kensho* (2006, pp. 57–58): *This turning about, this turning over, requires great energy. This is the work that has to be done.* Low, a Zen teacher of great experience, also quotes Dogen, another highly respected Zen master, in the context of effort (*op. cit.*, p. 58): *This sustained exertion is not something which people of the world naturally love or desire, yet it is the last refuge of all.* At the absolute level of no-mind, no effort is required, but as human beings enmeshed in a dualistic world, work is necessary. For that reason, the spiritual journey towards awakening requires effort as we, while in human form, move continuously forward towards the goal. For human beings to be free of misery, effort is required. We must exert ourselves to our utmost. The miracle is that we can do so when we have fully committed ourselves to it.

Breaking Free from the Trance of Everyday Life

To break free from the automatic, unconscious, deeply conditioned self-hypnosis of everyday life, we must recognize the painful and frustrating nature of our existence and stop deluding ourselves about the level of satisfaction we currently derive from our daily lives. We need to take stock of the ways, the frequency and the intensity with which we numb ourselves and medicate ourselves with ego-gratifying endeavors.

Imagine life in our modern world without compulsive behavior of all kinds. Could we surrender, even briefly, our dependence on cell phones, drugs, alcohol, gossip, mindless chatter, and our general aversion to silence? Have we become so dependent on whatever our preferred escape is that we cannot imagine life without it?

The most intractable, deep-seated, and unconscious addiction is to the idea of *me*. Ramana Maharshi, the great Indian sage who died in 1950, called it the *I-thought* (Godman, D., 1992, p. 53). If we're committed to the false belief that we're an enduring entity that is separate from other enduring entities, we cannot accomplish much in the journey towards awakening.

Creating Intimacy

If we listen carefully and objectively to anyone talk about anything for more than a few minutes, we will be startled at how self-centered the discussion is. Our human nature will be to judge what the other person is saying in one way or another. However, if we try to hear what they are saying without judgment, we create an opportunity to understand and appreciate the other person's unique perspective. This willingness to drop our automatic judgment and emotional reactivity provides for the possibility of real intimacy. It is human nature for us to interpret everything that happens in a self-referential manner. This process is so universal and automatic that we rarely notice it.

Our own narcissism is universal and dissolves only in the radical internal perceptual shift of a genuine awakening. This self-centered *I* is termed the ego. Awakening doesn't destroy the ego. Rather, there's a change in your internal relationship to this relentless, self-centered, obsessive self-preoccupation. It's the total identification *with* the self-identity that dissolves, not the self-identity itself.

Additionally, we experience a loss of interest in and attachment to the created, delusional fantasy about who we are. We can calmly observe the ego without identifying with it. There is a clear and unwavering awareness that our self-identity does have its own reality but is not all that we are at the deepest level. This irrefutable awareness is liberating. It then becomes possible to listen to other people without complete preoccupation with our own perceived self-interests. Only then can we have intimate, loving relationships that are not controlling and possessive. Only then can we give to others without concern for receiving.

Preferences Remain

After awakening we will still have preferences, likes and dislikes. The self-identity does not disappear completely while we are alive. However, we can learn to have a far more expansive understanding of who and what we are. The difference is that we no longer are compulsively addicted to our attachments and aversions. If we get what we want, there is the experience of enjoyment. If we do not get what we want, an almost instantaneous equanimity may arise along with the realization that the *not getting* is perfect also. This does not mean there is never a feeling of disappointment. Normal feelings also remain and are more transparent and easily accessible. There is a sometimes subtle underlying and continuous recognition that my getting what I want from life is not the most important experience I can have. Disappointment can be even more fruitful. I can remember many occasions where this was true for me. If your primary purpose in this life is to grow in spiritual truth and alignment, getting what you want is usually not beneficial!

There's nothing wrong with having attachments. Our attachments are part of what makes us fully human. With awakening, we do not stop caring about or loving those who are close to us. However, an internal shift in perception allows us to love and care for others without the intense dependency, jealousy, neediness, and possessiveness that typically characterizes even the best relationships. No matter how wonderful your life may appear to you, genuine freedom occurs only when there is a deep recognition of your true nature.

If we are to radically alter the quality of our life experience through an awakening, we must possess a passionate need to find another way of living our lives. We must expand our awareness of the opportunities available to us as human beings. We must believe that a more meaningful life is possible for everyone.

Faith

True faith arises from our own personal experience. Once we notice our increasing level of presence awareness, our faith in the reality of this way of life increases exponentially. Once we have even a brief taste of this direct knowing and clear seeing, we fully commit to the journey. Full awakening becomes the most important purpose of our life. Nothing else we could possibly do in this life will have such a beneficial impact on us.

Chapter Four

THE PRACTICE BEFORE AND AFTER AWAKENING

Shakyamuni Buddha has been practicing full time for the last 2500 years, and he's still only halfway there.
                                                    Zen Proverb

Awakening is to embrace what *is* so thoroughly that the ego of the one doing the embracing disappears into the experience of the moment. Life can then be enjoyed spontaneously in all its wonder and beauty. This natural unfolding happens by grace when we absolutely and involuntarily surrender. What are we surrendering? Think for a moment of how you spend your time every day. What are you doing? My impression from observing myself and others is that we spend our day trying to control what we have no control over. We try to control our own experience as well as the experience of others. So, what must be surrendered is the illusion of control.

We learn to live by trust in and intimacy with all that is, rather than by calculation, personal striving, and effort. We accept and recognize that all is perfect, just as it is. Nothing needs improving or changing in any way, including ourselves! Until now, our life had been one tedious self-improvement project after another. We believed that we were not okay exactly as we were. Resting quietly in this luminous awareness, we embrace and accept all that is. We return to the Source and discover who and what we really are and always have been.

Paradoxically this view does not negate the importance of accurately recognizing problems in our self and in the world and making sincere efforts to ameliorate suffering wherever we can. This seemingly dual view is the dialectic or ongoing tension between the world of form and the world of emptiness, to use the terms of the Heart Sutra. From the absolute view, all is perfect exactly as it is. From the relative view the world is full of overwhelming problems. Both perspectives are simultaneously true. The thinking mind cannot reconcile these seemingly opposite points of view. The resolution of this dichotomy occurs in a fully embodied awakening.

Rarely have individuals awakened deeply without any prior formal spiritual or meditative practice or discipline, although it certainly happens. For most of us, some form of spiritual practice both before and after awakening is vitally important. Any sincere spiritual practice gradually wears down our ego. Spiritual practice becomes much easier and more enjoyable, and we find ourselves relishing opportunities to decondition our mind's remaining beliefs, attachments and aversions. Some conditioned beliefs continue for all but the rarest spiritual geniuses. I have never personally known anyone like this, but possibly it applies to Jesus Christ or Shakyamuni, the historical Buddha, or others known and unknown.

For most of us struggling and suffering humans, the experience of realization can take years of practice. Be assured that regardless of how long it takes, no effort we make is wasted or unimportant. The more effort directed towards personal purification through the release of beliefs and assumptions before awakening, the easier it will be to live in the ordinary world and function well after this experience. Additionally, continuing our commitment to a personal spiritual practice makes it easier for us to carry out our responsibilities. We see with more clarity what is necessary and what is not.

Vasanas

Vasana is a Sanskrit term that refers to a past impression in the mind that influences behavior. It is often identified with the Advaita

Vedanta tradition and is very useful in helping us define and understand automatic, conditioned reactions.

Vasanas are quite subtle, subliminal, and persistent. They can include all conditioned and programmed mind activity, including thoughts, feelings, and bodily sensations. Our goal in observing and deprogramming our identity is to reduce the influence of vasanas, in order to reduce any unconscious conditioning which obscures our ability to see things as they are. The ultimate resolution is to act freely and spontaneously as a direct expression of our new ability to see clearly and know directly without the obscuring intervention of familial, social, cultural, linguistic and other forms of programming.

A goal can be defined as a target, aim, objective or destination. In short, a goal implies something that will happen in the future. This concept of a goal, of something that will happen at a time other than the present moment is anathema to aficionados of pure nonduality. They often identify with the neoadvaita movement in contemporary spiritual circles. However, while we live in a body, both duality and nonduality are real and important. To negate either is to miss the whole. Ultimately, both dual and nondual dissolve into *just this*. In *just this,* no *one* is speaking or acting and yet we do speak words, make decisions, act and pursue goals. There are some tools we can use to actively and deliberately reduce the effects of vasanas in our lives.

It has been my experience that the need for some form of spiritual practice does not end with awakening. Moreover, all deeply conditioned patterns and habits do not automatically disappear even after a deep awakening. Even within this continuous and unbroken direct awareness of reality, some conditioned habits and automatic reactions continue. In general, though, these reactions do not completely dominate post awakening behavior. Depending on the depth of self-realization, the awakened individual will usually notice the inner experience of distress prefacing unskillful behavior. With awareness and the intention to not continue with dysfunctional thoughts, feelings, sensations and behavior, it is possible to interrupt the previously automatic loop that led to further distress. I call this practice the ego deconstruction process. For those who wish to connect with their true nature, this practice will be invaluable in the integration and embodiment of awakened awareness in their daily life.

The Ego Deconstruction Process

The deconstruction of our identification with the limited sense of self begins with self-observation. The goal is to observe our internal experiences including thoughts, feelings, and sensations without automatically identifying with them. The phenomena of our thoughts, feelings and sensations are transient and ultimately meaningless. Our reactions to them are the direct result of arbitrary, capricious programming and conditioning. Self-observation with as much detachment and lack of critical judgment as possible is a powerful tool to help us recognize and deconstruct our most cherished assumptions.

SUGGESTED PRACTICE

Sit quietly and begin to observe the flow of thoughts, feelings, and sensations as they occur. Do not try to control this flow. Rather, simply observe the flow of your thoughts as if you were watching a movie. By carefully observing the content of the mind and body as thoughts, feelings and sensations spontaneously arise, we may become aware of the programming underneath. This programming is often in the form of beliefs and assumptions, but it can be other conditioned reactions including sensations, and feelings.

There is no goal to achieve from this process other than gradually developing skill at self-observation and becoming more conscious.

The ideal time to engage in this practice is when we are upset about something. If we are feeling this way when we begin this practice of self-observation, we need to simply observe ourselves being upset. Eventually we will notice how we create the feeling of being upset by the way we are thinking about an experience. How we experience anything is heavily determined by our way of perceiving and interpreting it. If we perceive differently, we change accordingly. Try to observe this relentless mental, emotional, and physiological process without comment or interpretation. If we find that we do comment on or otherwise interpret our experience, we simply need to notice that we are doing so.

There is no right or wrong here and no good or bad. The crucial step is to have the intention to observe ourselves impersonally without taking what we observe so seriously. It's a common misunderstanding and unrealistic to believe that the content of our minds is important. The truth is that thoughts, sensations and feelings themselves do not create mental anguish. Rather, our mental anguish is the direct result of the tendency to believe our conditioned perceptions, beliefs and reactions to be true. Over time and with repeated effort, witnessing the ongoing flow of our internal experience can help us develop an increasing detachment from our programming. We gradually realize that our beliefs and assumptions about reality are the result of conditioning and programming and, therefore, of no real consequence.

Thoreau's Meditation

The practice of self-observation is often identified with religious traditions that focus on formal meditation as a path to awakening. In the following passage from *Walden*, Henry David Thoreau gives a beautiful description of self-observation without any religious or spiritual overtones.

> *With thinking we may be beside ourselves in a sane sense. By a conscious effort of the mind, we can stand aloof from actions and their consequences; and all things, good and bad, go by us like a*

torrent. We are not wholly involved in Nature. I may be either the driftwood in the stream, or Indra in the sky looking down on it. I may be affected by a theatrical exhibition; on the other hand, I may not be affected by an actual event which appears to concern me much more. I only know myself as a human entity; the scene, so to speak, of thoughts and affections; and am sensible of a certain doubleness by which I can stand as remote from myself as from another. However intense my experience, I am conscious of the presence and criticism of a part of me, which, as it were, is not a part of me, but spectator, sharing no experience, but taking note of it, and that is no more I than it is you. When the play, it may be the tragedy, of life is over, the spectator goes his way. It was a kind of fiction, a work of the imagination only, so far as he was concerned. This doubleness may easily make us poor neighbors and friends sometimes.

Henry David Thoreau, Walden (2004, pp. 130-131).

The Practice of Daily Life

Eckhart Tolle and Byron Katie are contemporary teachers who appear to have awakened without any formal or informal spiritual practice. Dedicated spiritual practice is not always required because ordinary life provides a perfect crucible for the deconstruction of our self-identity. Catastrophic events or intense personal despair can push almost anyone over the edge and force a profound search for meaning as we are required to question previously accepted beliefs and assumptions. A fascinating historical account of a man who was pushed by catastrophe way beyond his ability to cope in ordinary ways is described in *The Way of a Pilgrim* (Pokrovsky, G., 2001). In this book, whose author is unknown, a young man tragically loses his wife and child in a house fire in 1850s Russia. He is burned but survives. Having lost everything, he sets out on foot with only a robe, a crucifix, a Bible and a loaf of bread determined to understand the meaning of St. Paul's injunction (First Thessalonians 5:17) to *pray without ceasing*. He searches far and wide before finding a monk who teaches him the correct practice of the Prayer of the Heart, or Jesus Prayer. This prayer is: *Lord Jesus Christ, Son of God, have mercy on me, a sinner*. It is said in coordination with the breath. See John Butler's book in the Bibliography for a description of this ancient practice still embraced in the Eastern Orthodox Christian tradition. Absent such a catastrophe that pushes us into self-deconstruction, there are three fundamental steps involved in the deliberate self-deconstruction process.

Three Steps to Self-Deconstruction

The first step in this process is becoming fully aware of the automatic, largely unconscious programming that normally controls our life. When observed dispassionately and objectively, we realize these patterns create needless problems and difficulties without providing any benefit to us. The next step teaches us how to lose interest in our programming. Much loss of interest is effortless and inevitable but can be facilitated by committing to certain practices. The third step involves an active effort to further identify and consciously deconstruct automatic assumptions and beliefs. These steps are not always experienced as sequential or discrete. For example, the observation, loss of interest and deconstruction aspects may occur simultaneously and without deliberate effort. They will be identified here individually to clarify their purpose.

In normal awareness, *we*, meaning who we take ourselves to be, identify completely with our ongoing flow of thoughts, feelings, and sensations. This identification is the root of our mental suffering. The beginning of freedom is the development of the natural ability to observe this continuous process without automatically identifying with it. Long periods of silent meditation can make it easier to develop this ability to observe. However, it is possible to develop this self-observation ability with or without the benefit of meditative practice. What's important to remember is that the more we learn to observe without identifying with the ceaseless flow of thoughts and other internal experiences, the more unencumbered we will be.

With continuous self-observation, it gradually becomes obvious that the content of our minds is tedious, boring, repetitive, and valueless. It is also largely unchanged from one day to the next. There's no reason to take any of it seriously. Yet, we are programmed to believe that because we *think* something, it must be true. Nothing could be further from the truth. Our continuous practice of self-observation will eventually reveal this fact to us.

Story Time

As we continue to practice observing the contents of our mind, we'll notice that we take this mindless, meaningless mental chatter far too seriously. In doing so, certain feelings and sensations will arise. We take ownership of them, and as such assume that these feelings and sensations are important because they appear to be happening to us. When we observe an inner feeling or sensation, we will almost invariably create a story in our mind that seems to help explain or justify what we are feeling or sensing. We believe that to do so is beneficial to us. We become very attached to the stories we create and are convinced they are true. We tend to forget that our stories about reality are not reality. They are, in fact, merely stories.

Our goal needs to be observing dispassionately this story-telling process as it unfolds. Over time, as our observing awareness is brought to inner experience, we begin to understand how we create these feelings and sensations by the way we think, interpret, and perceive. Our beliefs, assumptions, and expectations contribute much to our taking ownership of these feelings and sensations. We are programmed from birth to take it all very seriously. The beginning of real freedom occurs when we stop taking ourselves so seriously. We recognize our own mental chatter isn't nearly as important as we previously thought.

Feelings are Fine

We can observe feelings and bodily sensations with the same dispassionate curiosity that we have applied to our thoughts. For those on a serious spiritual path, there is often confusion about the best way to handle these feelings and sensations. Potentially disruptive emotional reactions are common experiences of those who are seriously pursuing a spiritual path. This is reasonable when we remember that the path of awakening involves becoming fully aware of automatic, conditioned reactions.

A primary purpose of conditioning is to allow us to become emotionally numb and, thereby, more comfortable with inauthentic behaviors in others and ourselves. As our ability to see and know what is real progressively expands, this protective numbing wears away, leaving us less buffered, more open, less defended. The more we can recognize and embrace what is real, the more intimate we become with all that is. This increased openness to all experience, which is also called *presence*, is wonderful and is an aspect of what we are seeking.

Spiritual Bypassing

However, as conditioned reactions and their attendant numbing diminish, emotional and physical side effects may well emerge as an inevitable part of this process. One effective way to manage such reactions is through engaging in spiritual practices. However, we need to guard against becoming overly reliant on these practices. While they are helpful, they can also become powerful defenses against full awakening. They are also not a substitute for psychotherapy, body work, medical care or other healing modalities, all of which have great potential value and may be needed at times.

Spiritual practices and even the interpretation given to glimpses of awakening may be used to avoid emotional pain and suffering. *Spiritual bypassing* describes the deliberate or inadvertent use of spiritual practices and beliefs to avoid facing painful feelings or unresolved emotional wounds. This process is extensively described in the book *Spiritual Bypassing: When Spirituality Disconnects Us from What Really Matters* by psychologist Robert Augustus Masters (2010). While it is true that most people come to intensive spiritual practice because of a wish to better manage emotional or physical pain, the direct path is to go into the pain, not away from it. The Way is always to embrace reality as it is, not to transcend, avoid or deny painful truths. At the same time, a genuine spiritual quest reveals the nuances of how we needlessly create, even manufacture, much of our experienced pain and suffering. This process is the result of programming and conditioning and is largely inevitable until we become more aware of our true nature. We cannot control the world or other people, but we can certainly learn to be fully present for what is real. If there is a mantra needed, let it be: Just this, only this, but really *this*!

Anger, resentment, jealousy, contempt, desire, and aversion are normal aspects of the human experience, yet these and other negative feelings are sometimes hard to reconcile with Buddhist, Christian, Advaita and other traditional religious teachings on compassion and forgiveness. We are encouraged to refrain from judging others, yet brief experiences with self-observation of ongoing mental content reveal an unending stream of these judgments. There is nothing wrong with any of this. It is just the way we and all other humans have operated for millennia. By carefully observing this process we can begin to be free of it.

Our self-observation practice encourages us to focus on becoming aware of and radically accepting of our entire experience, exactly as it is, without judgment, suppression, denial or avoidance. Negative thoughts and feelings will spontaneously arise. These experiences are a normal part of the functioning of the conditioned mind, and as such, they are not particularly important. Learning to observe these inner experiences with tolerance, acceptance, mild curiosity, and lack of judgment is a necessary first step in releasing the grip they can have on us.

Once these experiences come into full awareness, much of the energy that fuels them naturally dissipates without any extra effort on our part. Seeing things directly as they are is often all that we need to do. This practice of recognizing and embracing our experience fully, exactly as it is, needs to be our primary focus. However, try to keep in mind that particularly sticky, deeply ingrained patterns of belief and conditioned reactions may require more direct and formal intervention, such as direct work with a teacher or psychotherapist who is aware of the potential pitfalls of the spiritual path. The true path is always to look inward, facing ourselves directly, and embracing all that we are-the good, the bad, even the ugly. Nothing can be omitted, left out, or excluded. There is really no place to hide.

It can help to write down realizations that spontaneously emerge as this process continues. We need to make special note to observe the content of our minds when we are upset. We may find that the very moment we begin to dispassionately observe the contents of our mind, our mood will lighten, and we will feel less upset. An internal space is created in us which allows for an experience of freedom and possibility.

Remembrance

It's important to remember as often as possible during the day to self-observe and witness. We are not simply trying to change ourselves. Rather, we are trying to accept ourselves exactly as we are. Nothing needs to be any different from what it is right now. We are merely bringing the light of neutral, objective awareness to previously automatic, unconscious beliefs and assumptions that have done nothing but create suffering for us. Most of these pernicious beliefs and assumptions are universal and impersonal. Neutral self-observation is our ticket out of this endless cycle of self-created suffering.

It's important that we repeat this practice on a regular basis. Repetition of the practice leads to liberation from the mental anguish we suffer from believing our thoughts and sensations to be true. Repeating the practice of self-observation moves us towards awareness as opposed to bogging our minds down with more beliefs. We will notice, almost immediately, very positive changes in ourselves if we actively commit to practicing self-observation.

Automatic Beliefs and Unconscious Assumptions

An important part of the ego deconstruction process involves ferreting out and deprogramming unquestioned beliefs and assumptions. It is invaluable to become consciously aware of some of the deeply held, automatic assumptions by which we live our lives. Once we become more aware of these automatic beliefs, it is valuable for us to ask whether continuing to believe they are valid is necessary and beneficial for us. It may be hard even to begin to identify our own assumptions, as they are often largely unconscious. One way of becoming aware of these assumptions is to ask ourselves: What kinds of beliefs would cause us to think and act the way we do?

Worry: Who Needs It?

Worry appears to be a nearly universal human experience. When examined carefully, it is apparent that worry is never useful and always emotionally draining. It therefore begs the question: Why do we continue to worry?

SUGGESTED PRACTICE

Take a moment now to recollect experiences in your life when you vividly imagined horrific events unfolding. Ask yourself these questions and write down your answers for your own personal reflection:

Did the bad experiences unfold because you imagined them?
Was it beneficial for you to worry about them?
Is it necessary to worry in order to be a responsible adult?
Are you drained, depleted and upset when you worry?
Is it beneficial for you to continue to worry?
Can you permit yourself to let go of the habit of worrying?
What would it feel like to not worry?
Would you become irresponsible if you stopped worrying?
How do you think your life would change?
Does not worrying sound appealing?
What are the unconscious beliefs you have that contribute to your worry?
Write down some of your own deeply held, automatic assumptions and convictions.

Mistaken Assumptions

We are programmed to believe we should worry. Behind this belief is a conviction that we might be able to prevent bad outcomes in the future if we do so. Here are a few of the mistaken assumptions we are programmed to believe:

- We assume worrying is the mark of a mature, responsible adult.
- We assume worrying means we care about other people.
- We assume worrying means we are supporting people in their struggles.
- We assume worrying is one way we show our love for others.
- We assume worrying is a productive use of our time if there is no action we can take to resolve whatever conflict has us worried.
- We assume worrying helps us think through a future course of action and, thereby, reduce the potential for mistakes.
- We assume worrying makes us feel less helpless.
- We assume all the responsible people we have known have worried, so it must be useful.
- We assume that if we do not worry, we will seem uncaring and lacking in compassion to others.

In every case, we assume wrong. The real question is: Does worrying ever help?

It's time to take full responsibility for ourselves. No one is responsible for our feelings other than us. Our parents inculcated social norms and beliefs in us, and they did that job to the best of their ability, believing that passing on cultural norms is necessary and beneficial. Of course, it is important to learn the norms of our culture. We have also received this conditioning from friends, teachers, other relatives, religious instructors or coaches. However, as adults it is our choice as to whether we will allow these programmed beliefs to control and torment us. We will need to discern which norms benefit us and which norms do not. We need to take the time to reflect on the convictions that control our behavior. In so doing, we will acquire a new and invaluable self-awareness.

Chapter Five

SURRENDER SEEKING AND FIND

*To seek Great Mind with thinking mind
is certainly a grave mistake.*

Affirming Faith in Mind
(*Daily Chants and Recitations*, 2005, p. 28)

Living continuously in accord with our true nature is possible for each of us. It is our purpose.

When we live in accordance with our own true nature, we live in presence awareness. This state is the actual personal experience of living in the presence of God, or whatever word is comfortable for you to use to define a Higher Power. God is never separate from us, as we are always one with our Higher Power. We cannot be separate from our creator, no matter how hard we might try. In John 8:58, Jesus speaks directly from this ground of Being:

> '*Very truly I tell you,*' Jesus answered, '*before Abraham was born, I am!*'

This I AM is who we always have been and can't not be. The intuitive realization and behavioral expression of the I AM is an answer to the Zen koan: *Show me your original face before your parents were born.*

A Personal Goal of Waking Up

Awakening to our true nature always happens through unfathomable, unearned grace. It is unpremeditated and strikes in the most wondrous, unforeseen manner-when our normal, thinking, ruminating mind is offline. As the Apostle Paul remarked in 1 Thessalonians 5:2

> *for you know very well that the day of the Lord will come like a thief in the night.*

Knowing this, we must nevertheless do everything we can to facilitate God's grace. This recognition immediately propels us into the question of grace versus personal effort. Both are important and both appear to be required. Awakened awareness is present fully all the time, yet its recognition requires prodigious effort. In one sense, there's nothing to work at or strive to achieve or recognize, because *it* is already here. Yet it's also true that we mostly don't recognize what's right in front of us.

Our ordinary world of form, duality and differentiation involves genuine satisfaction and enjoyment, as well as suffering. True liberation is not the result of denying the ordinary world, where up is always different from down, and some actions are compassionate while others are malicious and harmful. We don't need to deny what's real. The outcome of diligent spiritual work is to see reality as it is, not to escape from it.

To be fully present is to be open to all levels of reality and to live simultaneously in form and non-form. In full awareness of what is, we perceive form continuously through its underlying aspect of formlessness. We see clearly and with equanimity when form and formlessness aren't two.

This sounds hopelessly abstract, and words are clumsy vehicles to convey this realization. However, it's possible to describe the experience of living in this total oneness of form and formlessness. It's doing without a doer, acting without an actor, and thinking without a thinker.

Seeking

> *1 And he said: Whoever finds the correct*
> *Interpretation of these sayings will never die.*
> *2 Jesus said: The seeker should not stop until he*
> *finds. When he does find, he will be disturbed. After*
> *having been disturbed, he will be astonished.*
> *Then he will reign over everything.*
>
> The Gospel of Thomas

Jesus directs us to seek until we find. Are seeking and finding, in fact, different? How do we seek in a way that might lead to finding?

In Matthew 7:7 Jesus says,

> *Ask and it will be given to you, seek and you will find, knock and the door will be opened to you. For everyone who asks receives, he who seeks finds, and to him who knocks, the door will be opened.*

Be assured: of those few who find, all sought first. You must truly seek with all your heart, all your mind, and all your spirit.

In the *Mumonkan*, the classic book of Zen koans compiled in the 13th century by Zen Master Mumon, we find Case # 12, *Zuigan Calls 'Master.'* The challenge is presented:

> *Every day Master Zuigan would call out to himself, 'Oh, Master!' and would answer himself 'Yes?' 'Wake up, wake up!' he would*

> *cry, and would answer 'Yes, yes!' 'Don't be deceived by others, at any time, day or night.' 'No, I will not.'*

Once again, this begs the question, *Are there really two?* Seeking in a persistent, determined manner, the kind of seeking that might even lead to finding, does not come easy. Like Zuigan, we might say to ourselves, *Remember to seek! Stay present! Be vigilant! Pay attention! Time flies by! Death could come at any time!* And answer confidently, *Oh, don't worry; I will!* In my work as a psychotherapist, I'm often told, *I'm having trouble staying present.* I usually say something like, *Really? Where else could you be besides right here?* A Zen master might ask, *Who is the one that is trying to stay somewhere?*

Confusion is the stock and trade of a serious seeker after truth. Do we want to be comfortable and feel in control? If so, we are in the wrong place. We cannot enter the Kingdom with our beliefs intact.

Affirming Faith in Mind is the touchstone to which I repeatedly return. It states:

> *In this true world of Emptiness both self and other are no more……the wise in all times and places awaken to this primal truth.*
>
> *To enter this true empty world, immediately affirm "not-two"….*
> *…. Not only here, not only there, truth's right before your very eyes.*
> Daily Chants and Recitations (2005, p. 30.)

A calling one and one who answers; one who seeks and one who finds. One who previously sought, but now has found.

The question arises: *But what do I do?*

Somehow, we must summon the courage or desperation to slay our deepest attachments. Like Arjuna in *The Bhagavad Gita*, terrified and totally freaked out, we must pick up the sword of truth and wisdom and deconstruct all that we know and believe we are. The real miracle is that we can do what is required. We must seek, however, in order to find. Jesus instructs us to seek. We must knock for the door to open. A passionate need to know is required. However, having sought the truth with all our heart, mind, and spirit, we must somehow give up seeking or, rather, be given up by the seeking.

To find we must be willing and prepared to give up everything we hold dear. Being a spiritual seeker is far different from being a finder. Being a seeker doesn't threaten or destabilize the ordinary mind and its compulsive activity and self-absorption. Finding, however, destabilizes everything. Comfort and security, so treasured by most, are not the friend of the true seeker.

False Concepts of Awakening

We may have preconceived notions of how an enlightened person should look or act, but awakening is nothing we can picture. Therefore, any concepts of what it might be or look like are useless to us.

Enlightened people have always come in all shapes, colors, and sizes. Nisargadatta Maharaj (1999) not only smoked cigarettes, but also made his living selling tobacco. Some enlightened individuals eat meat; others don't. Some drink alcohol or are sexually active; others abstain entirely from alcohol and sex. Awakening has nothing to do with whether we engage in certain activities or not.

Some awakened individuals do not actively identify with any religious tradition, although they may have embraced traditional religious paths prior to their experience of awakening. This happens because in clear seeing the truth is revealed to not exclusively reside in any religious tradition.

That said, it was my own personal experience that I could lovingly embrace Christianity, the religion of my childhood, only after my shift in awareness. I could understand Buddhist and Christian scriptures only after this deeper realization. All religious traditions have typically strayed far from the simple, bare truth originally presented by their founder. It appears to me that religions are created not by the spiritual genius who inspired the new religion, but by ordinary men and women who often have very little intuitive understanding of the revelations at the heart of the teaching. That is why religions are characterized by rules and regulations, prohibitions and prescriptions for behavior. At the same time, the directly realized Truth discussed in this book is consistent with the fundamental awareness proposed by the founders of the world's great religions. My realization made it possible to embrace the fullness of Christianity and Buddhism.

The direct, experiential realization in our current body-mind of who we are is awakening to our true nature. The immediate result of this realization is that we're able for the first time to see reality as it is, rather than as we have perceived it to be. The inner experience of this recognition of things as they are is absolute freedom.

This Body and Mind

We believe that the sense of personal identity is critically important. We also believe that our physical body and our thinking mind define who we are. Descartes' maxim *I think, therefore I am* is taken for granted to be obviously true.

We believe that the content of our thoughts and feelings matters. We are burdened by many fixed, unconscious, deeply conditioned beliefs and assumptions that severely restrict our freedom and autonomy. An example is the belief that we should never offend anyone. It has become popular, even *de rigueur* in some circles, to become offended very easily. In truth how we feel is our responsibility. Our feelings are not dependent on the behavior of other's, but on our interpretation of their behavior. This is a crucial distinction. Anyone at any time can be offended by anything said or unsaid. Yet in our current world, the mere fact that people believe that they have been offended is enough to create major repercussions. To move through the world in accord with our true nature, we must question every assumption and every belief we have. All our beliefs are the direct result of prior programming and conditioning. Ordinarily, we never question our beliefs and assumptions, but to wake up to what is real, we must begin to question everything. No one has ever experienced true awakening without going through this radical transformation in some manner.

Is Effort Necessary?

Albert Low says (*op. cit.,* p. 56),

> *Without exertion, no turnabout is possible. The extent of the turnabout is dependent on the work that we do. If we do a little work, a little turnabout occurs; if we do intense work, a great turnabout occurs; if we do no work, no turnabout occurs. What we have to do is bring ourselves constantly back to the center of this work.*

In Matthew 7:13–14, Jesus instructs us:

> *Enter through the narrow gate. For wide is the gate and broad is the road that leads to destruction, and many enter through it. But small is the gate and narrow the road that leads to life, and only a few find it.*

Of the few who find, most had to search with all their heart and mind and spirit. To find, we must first seek. The gate Jesus describes is no gate at all. Passing through this gateless gate, we change beyond recognition.

> *And he said: Whoever finds the correct interpretation of these sayings will never die. Jesus said: The seeker should not stop until he finds. When he does find, he will be disturbed. After having been disturbed, he will be astonished. Then he will reign over everything.*
>
> The Gospel of Thomas, (Davies, S., 2003, p. 3.)

While some contemporary awakened teachers appear on the surface to have done very little formal spiritual practice to awaken, closer inspection reveals many years of intense, consuming, although not necessarily spiritual effort prior to awakening.

Satyam Nadeen (2000) describes how he pursued spiritual realization relentlessly through a deep and committed involvement with various spiritual teachers and practices. In other words, his life was devoted to the sincere pursuit of this truth. However, apparently nothing much changed until he was committed to a county jail for two years and then a maximum-security federal prison for two more years for sale of the drug Ecstasy. His realization, which occurred early in his confinement, appears to have been triggered by reading Ramesh Balsekar, an Advaita Vedanta teacher in the lineage of Ramana Maharshi (*From Onions to Pearls*, 1999).

People do have genuine awakenings that are profound and lasting without any apparent spiritual practice beforehand. It would be reasonable to say that their practice was the depth and profundity of the suffering that consumed them. While we can acknowledge that such awakenings do happen, it would be folly to wait around for similar lightning to strike us. Conscious, deliberate practice is necessary for most of us to have any hope of seeing clearly.

No one can tell us what we need to do to awaken. It's unique and unpredictable for all those who go through it. The one commonality is a total giving up, an absolute involuntary surrender of the ego, which then precipitates the beginning of radical internal change. Contemporary awakened teachers who may appear to us to have made little conscious, deliberate effort to awaken have all been engaged in a fierce and prolonged struggle, something like the effort required by a moth to break free of the cocoon. Without this intense effort over many years, they would not have acquired the requisite strength and resilience that's necessary to break through their inability to see and to then function in their new awareness.

Ethical Behavior

The more there has been a reduction of ego-based beliefs prior to awakening, the easier it will be after that experience for us to honor our responsibilities and function in the world. Thus, the classic injunction of all organized religions to live an ethical, upright life is also highly effective for one on the path to awakening. Dr. David Hawkins (2002) reminds us of the value of a commonsense regard for others, as in the Golden Rule, the Ten Commandments, and the Boy Scout Oath. These and other time-honored, traditional codes of behavior can be valuable to the dedicated spiritual student. It would be perilous for us to ignore this; to do so is to give energy and power to our ego.

As obvious as it may sound, one of the best spiritual practices is to avoid evil and do what is right, to paraphrase a point made by David Hawkins (Hawkins, D., 2002). The Dalai Lama and many other genuine spiritual teachers encourage acting with loving kindness to all creatures without exception and without thought of personal gain. Treating others with respect and dignity is an example of fully awakened behavior. In the Zen Buddhist tradition at the end of an arduous seven-day silent retreat, the tradition is to dedicate the spiritual merit acquired through one's efforts to Buddhist teachers of the past. The karmic merit of any activity is understood to multiply many times for the practitioner when the disciplined practice occurs without any thought of personal gain.

The Role of Faith

> *With single mind one with the Way,*
> *All ego-centered strivings cease;*
> *Doubts and confusion disappear,*
> *and so true faith pervades our life.*

Affirming Faith in Mind
(op. cit., p. 29-30, 2005)

True faith is not a decision to believe in concepts and fantasies. Rather, it is created by hard work, effort, and a willingness to do whatever is necessary to realize the truth of what *is*. Real faith sustains us through the long, barren and parched periods that inevitably occur in serious spiritual practice.

There are two basic forms of real faith. The first and most powerful is the faith that is the direct result of our own experiences. Personally, I have always felt grateful and fortunate to have experienced an initial spontaneous awakening in January of 1982. This gift of the spirit aroused my deep faith in the truth and reality of Buddhist teachings.

Others have had spontaneous awakenings that occurred outside the context of any religious teaching. How we interpret our experience is conditioned by our beliefs and concepts and is independent of any tradition or belief system.

The second kind of true faith comes from exposure to a real teacher who can demonstrate and manifest awakened awareness in speech and action. I was fortunate to have met Roshi Philip Kapleau who was that real teacher for me. Absent the option of a real teacher, true faith can sometimes be ignited by reading the works of awakened teachers, hearing their recorded talks, or watching their videos.

A wonderful example of deep faith formed from personal experience can be found in "Master Hakuin's Chant in Praise of Zazen" (*Daily Chants and Recitations*, 2005, p. 35):

> *This earth where we stand is the pure Lotus Land,*
> *And this very body the body of Buddha.*

This earth, exactly as it is, is truly perfect if we can see clearly. The Garden of Eden is not far away in time and space. It is right before our very eyes. Similarly, we are whole and complete exactly as we are. We don't need to become anything other than who we already are. Seeing this truth for ourselves is the real challenge.

Faith as we commonly understand it is a personal acceptance of a series of ideas and beliefs without proof of their veracity. This form of faith is shallow and crumbles easily under pressure. For example, consider the concept that Mary, the mother of Jesus, is a virgin when the Holy Spirit impregnates her. We cannot accept this idea in any other way than blind faith. Obviously, we cannot know whether Mary was in fact a virgin when impregnated by the Holy Spirit, and the idea of it seems far-fetched and against the grain of common sense. We probably would reject it immediately except for faith. Faith, as usually understood, then, means a willing, conscious, ego-based suspension of our willingness to think critically and come to our own conclusions. In this kind of faith, we are deciding that someone or some group knows what is real and we do not.

We accept so much on faith of this sort that we rarely stop to question its value. Do we benefit from believing in concepts and ideas that we don't personally know to be true? In the case of the mother of Jesus, does whether she was a virgin matter in terms of the real point of the Jesus story? I certainly do not have the answers to these questions, but I am skeptical of assuming the veracity of beliefs that I cannot personally verify. Of course, we are each free to make up our own minds about such matters.

Direct Knowing

For me it appears that I either know or don't know. If I know it is because knowledge was spontaneously revealed. If information has not been revealed to me, then I don't know. I have no interest in speculating based solely on beliefs and assumptions. When asked any question it is immediately apparent that I either know or don't know. If I know then I say what I know. When I know I answer with confidence. This is because what I know did not emerge from my personal thinking. Consequently, I have no doubt of the truth of the knowing. The information that arises from this direct knowing is very powerful and cuts through illusion.

I have at times been accused of arrogance by those whose only way of knowing is through the very limited and often distorted conventional channels of the thinking mind. What may appear to be arrogance is actually a profound humility. I know nothing until it is revealed to me. Once I know it would be wrong to pretend I don't know, or to answer with a fake uncertainty. Conversely, I have no difficulty saying I don't know. If I don't know I assume it is because there is no need for me to know. Therefore, I am fine with not knowing. I am not in charge of this process. The Holy Spirit shows me directly what I need to know, and I am totally content with what I am shown. I have no need to know what I don't know, and I generally have little to no curiosity about that which I do not know. None of this discussion of knowing would have made any sense to me prior to the spiritual transformation in 2002. If it does not make sense to you now, that is fine. Allow yourself not to know. You do not need to know something you do not yet know!

Awakening means the absolute and total surrender of all beliefs, assumptions, and convictions. This surrender is not conscious, deliberate, ego-driven, or voluntary. It is rare and appears to occur on its own for no discernable reason. It happens outside of linear causality, as we usually understand it, and any firmly held beliefs interfere with the spontaneous appearance of this profound form of grace.

The good news is that after some genuine glimpse of the truth, however fleeting the glimpse may be, the real spiritual journey begins, changing our lives forever. Once we have seen for ourselves, we know. With genuine knowing we have no need for beliefs. Once we have seen for ourselves, we *know* for certain and do not need beliefs. This knowing, based solidly on our own experience, is irrefutable. In this awakening to what is real, questions disappear. In the Gospel of John 8:32, Jesus says:

> *You will know the truth,*
> *And the truth will make you free.*

No problems or concerns exist in the state of pure presence awareness. Everything and everyone are perfect, not in the sense of the self-identity or the body, but perfect in the sense that nothing needs to change to be fully and completely itself. In awakening, there is a lack of interest in creating imaginary realities and then pretending that these illusions are real. There is also a realization that critical judgments of self and others are needless and serve no purpose other than to cause separation, frustration and stress.

Silence

Periods of silence can be extremely valuable in accessing no-mind accessing no-mind awareness. Maintaining external silence encourages the development of internal silence. Spiritual transformation can occur only when the thinking mind is momentarily silent.

When we are quiet and able to focus on the workings of our own minds, we will inevitably become aware of how *noisy* our minds really are. The noise in our minds is the result of our thoughts. We identify with this mental noise and believe it is real and important. We believe erroneously that this incessant mental chatter is who we really are. To simply notice this noise, without judgment and without believing it to be true, is the best practice for awakening. As you become progressively quieter and still, notice if there is a part of you that seems frightened. Remember Descartes maxim, *I think, therefore I am*. What if you are so quiet that no thoughts occur? Do you still exist?

Silence, especially in the context of a spiritual retreat, creates an extraordinary opportunity to see how trivial and meaningless our usual mental busyness is. By continuously paying attention to this obsessive and relentless fantasizing, judging, and worrying, we eventually become sick and tired of it and ultimately let go of it. In Zen terms, this is called *dropping body and mind*.

Being miserable is neither necessary nor beneficial. When we lose interest in our mind and its content, an entirely new and unfamiliar world opens. To lose interest in our mind is to surrender in the deepest sense of the word. It is only then that *not my will, but Thy will be done* makes sense. Our goal should be nothing less than to realize our full potential as a human being by letting go of who and what we have always thought we were. The purpose of a true spiritual path is to disappear into the Mind of Christ, Buddha Mind, All That Is, resting in the sense of presence. By simply doing nothing, going nowhere, becoming nothing, we have an opportunity to rest deeply in the presence of God.

Freedom

We cannot be who we believe we should be and be free. We cannot be who our parents, the church, our spouse, our kids, or our employer wants us to be and be free. We must seek freedom *from* ourselves, instead of freedom to *be* ourselves. *That* is the definition of real freedom.

Awakening usually involves the often-painful realization of all the myriad ways we have imprisoned ourselves. Becoming truly free reveals clearly to us how profoundly numb and detached we have been throughout our lives.

The very good news is that we don't have to continue to imprison ourselves in our own conditioned beliefs. The cell door has always been open for us to walk through. There really is no barrier to our freedom. Developing a spiritual practice as described in this book is the first step towards true freedom. In this freedom we become one with the presence of God in all things and all situations. This oneness completely fulfills the Apostle Paul's injunction to pray without ceasing. In effect, our life becomes a living prayer as everything is continuously surrendered to the Creator.

Chapter Six

AN INTERNAL PERCEPTUAL SHIFT

*The Mind that wakes up
is the same Mind that went to sleep.*

An accurate description of this internal shift in perception is challenging at best. When we awaken to our true nature, we see that it's no nature at all. In pure, direct awareness, we see reality as it is. It's all so very simple yet can be incredibly challenging to personally realize.

Any description of this new awareness must be provisional, tentative, and indirect. For example, imagine the finger pointing at the moon as opposed to the moon itself. No description is completely accurate. In fact, the best description is no verbal description. Observing an awakened teacher's behavioral demonstration of the awakened mind's engagement with the ordinary world of form best conveys this understanding.

Transmission

Through an energetic resonance between teacher and student, a transmission of no-mind awareness or Mind may occur. This energetic communion is said to be outside of words and letters. It is also true that nothing at all is transmitted. The teacher has nothing to give that we don't already have, yet a real teacher's physical presence is invaluable at kindling the recognition of awareness already present but not noticed. Perhaps it is now clear why nothing is gained in awakening. There is only the loss of our mistaken sense of separation from all that is. For the experience of transmission to occur, the mind of the spiritual student must be silent. The development and cultivation of this internal stillness is the purpose of all spiritual practice. Only when the student's mind is still and without the ripples of thought can an awareness of what *is* spontaneously arise.

Mind

I was not involved in formal Zen training when the enduring shift in consciousness happened for me in 2002. Previously, I had worked closely with two authentic Zen teachers, and once that connection is made, it is never broken. The connection to which I refer is not a to a specific person, but rather to no-mind itself manifested through a human being. This Mind is present equally everywhere, forever, unchanging. We are better able to recognize this Mind, which is our *own* mind, when the form of another human being, most especially an awakened teacher expresses and demonstrates it.

When I use the word Mind, I use it interchangeably with the word no-mind or God. I do not understand God to be separate from or outside of me, Mind, no-mind awareness or the entire universe. God or Mind is not *other*. God is not hidden. We cannot be separate from or outside of God, even if we try. I was shown directly that we cannot fall out of the grace of God. When we imagine that God is *other*, meaning somehow fundamentally different from us, we create a needless act of separation between our self and the Divine Creator of all that is. Only with this misunderstanding of separation can we name God. This is why in orthodox Judaism G_D is not named. To name is to define and limit. The Divine Creator of Heaven and Earth cannot be defined, limited or even described. *It* simply *is*. Yet God is continuously revealed in the smallest detail of everyday life. It is our job to learn to see this truth for our self. Do not take my word for it. Open your eyes and see for yourself.

Not only here not only there
Truth's right before your very eyes.
Affirming Faith in Mind, (p. 30, op. cit.)

The Direct Path to Self-Realization

Being fully human is the direct path. We don't have to become different or better in some way. It is usually not necessary to lose weight, stop smoking, stop drinking alcohol, give up drugs, meditate more, become celibate or vegetarian. All of these actions may be beneficial for the health of the body and mind, but they do not necessarily facilitate self-realization, and they certainly are not requirements in general. However, everyone is unique and if you have the sense you should change your life in some way, please do so. There are very few if any absolutes, and rules and regulations do not apply. Question deeply and find out for yourself what is ultimately true for you.

Everything in this book is at best a pointer and provisional, although it does represent my own effort to clarify what seems to be true for me. For example, there are many instances of active substance addicts waking up while still addicted. They became sober because of the clear seeing resulting from their awakening. There are probably many other instances of people who had to become sober first before they could awaken. If you are alive you are a candidate for awakening. Let nothing deter you. Our true nature is already present, right here, right now. It can't be anywhere else.

Total engagement with daily life, with what *is*, is the straight and narrow path. No one can walk it for us. The path that leads directly to the total dissolution of everything we currently believe we are may seem too difficult, but there are others who have had the same fear and yet have awakened. To have this experience is the end of the sense of separation.

When I experienced my own fear of dissolution, of disappearing, Roshi Phillip Kapleau suddenly appeared in front of me and said, *You can't fall out of the universe.* Roshi Kapleau's appearance before me was not in the form of a physical body, but rather an energetic body. Hearing those words set me free to let go and die to who and what I had always believed I was. Hearing did not occur with my physical ears but with my entire being. That is why it was so powerful and created a profound trust and reassurance that whatever I truly was would not be harmed by this ultimate letting go. This experience, while not yet deep enough to be a real awakening or *kensho* in the Zen tradition, was nevertheless life altering.

Dead Men Walking

> *Jesus said to her, 'He who believes in me will live, even though he dies.'*
>
> John 11:25

What does Jesus mean here? These are challenging and confusing words, especially if taken in a concrete manner. However, as with everything Jesus says in his relatively brief time on this earth, these words are valuable pointers towards ultimate truth and have depth and richness.

Jesus does not literally mean we have to only believe in something we cannot know to be true. Belief ungrounded in direct experience is shallow and fragile. Only when we let go of all our beliefs can we *know*. Beliefs are merely ego-based constructs. The mistaken belief that we can know the truth of our being with our thinking mind leads to the idea that some beliefs are correct and others incorrect. The usual corollary is that our beliefs are correct, and those who disagree with us are wrong. However, if we give up trying to know anything at all, we move closer to reality. The mind that knows is closed; the mind that does not know is open to knowing. A beneficial practice is to assume that you do not know anything. When asked virtually any question, it can be liberating to say, "I do not know". Learn to welcome and embrace not knowing. It is your true home.

Belief, as Jesus uses it in this passage, means to know. If we truly know what is real, then birth and death will mean little to us. To know Jesus in this manner is to know God, which is to know our true self, which is no-self.

It is good when our thinking mind runs aground. When the thinking mind seizes up, stalls and quits, an opening is created for awareness to flood into the space now revealed to be silent, still and empty. Eventually we realize that the awareness that is our true nature has always been here, and that there is no space that needs to open. We recognize that our self-identity, like our body, is finite. When our body dies, so dies the self-identity. As long as the body lives, we will also have a seeming self-identity. The correct path is to gradually lose interest in this created sense of an independent self. There is no problem here. When our body dies, all false constructs die with it. Our true self, however, lives forever, from before time and through all eternity. With body and mind dropped, what remains? Only the birthless and deathless one, which is our true nature.

How Do We Recognize Our True Nature?

Life and death are two sides of the same coin. Our goal when alive is to be fully alive; when dead, fully and completely dead. We don't want to be a ghost wandering on this earth endlessly seeking for who knows what. The question then, is how do we fully live the life of a human being?

> *Step One*
> Recognize how rarely you are *alive* and fully present to what is real.

Step Two
Recall past experiences in which you were wide-awake, present and open to whatever was occurring. As you recall those experiences, ask these questions:
1) What were the qualities being truly alive?
2) How did you feel emotionally, physically and energetically when you felt most alive?
3) When experiencing this degree of alive presence, did something happen that seemed to precipitate the experience?
4) How could you return to this experience again?
5) Is being fully alive your goal in life? If not, why not?

When we are anxious, worried, and troubled, the lack of basic self-acceptance of who we really are and what is real is usually at the root of our problems. We live in a fantasy world that tells us we can avoid problems by worrying about them ahead of time. We falsely believe we can make our emotional truth conform to what our conditioned, programmed mind thinks and believes.

One very important aspect of becoming one with the Way of Life is to accept our emotional and physical reality as it is. We must accept ourselves as we are without shame, remorse, or regret. This radical self-acceptance lies at the core of the spiritual path. We do not need to be something other than what we already are.

For example, we read that being significantly overweight creates all manner of health problems over time. This, of course, can be true. Being obese, and especially morbidly obese, carries major health risks. However, as a clinical psychologist, I have listened to people verbally and emotionally abuse themselves about weight and other issues for more than forty years. At this point, whenever a client starts to express these automatic, deeply conditioned self-judgments, I intervene to stop the litany of self-abuse. Nothing beneficial will come of it.

Forgo Self-Judgment

People often judge themselves very harshly for their inability to change some self-destructive behavior. Intense self-judgment impedes any real change in their behavior because harsh self judgement is a defense mechanism employed to prevent the judgement of others. The individual is subconsciously saying to themselves, *If I emotionally abuse myself about my lack of change, then you have no right to be critical of me also.*

This is a self-defeating pattern. This tremendous self-criticism subconsciously gives us permission to not change. There is also an underlying belief that by severely criticizing myself, I can avoid criticism from others for not changing my self-destructive behavior. These are examples of the kind of largely unconscious beliefs and assumptions that are not only unhelpful but create needless suffering without facilitating beneficial change. By sitting quietly in a curious, open awareness, these destructive beliefs will often surface naturally for examination and eventual deconstruction.

We can begin to help ourselves change by facing reality. We can see that our current self-destructive behaviors have never served us well, and to continue engaging in those behaviors will serve no useful purpose. We can pay attention to our thoughts, sensations and feelings, and especially to any self-hating thoughts and judgments. Then, we can begin to pay attention to the very painful feelings that follow in the wake of such thoughts. Next, we become aware of the subsequent drop in energy level and enthusiasm for making any effort towards change that inevitably follows from believing in negative thoughts. Realizing the spiral downwards these negative thoughts, feelings and judgements can generate, we can make a choice to not engage in them any longer. Choosing healthy, positive, constructive thoughts, feelings and observations whenever possible will facilitate a less conflicted and unhappy life immediately.

It is easy to understand why we could feel despair about the possibility of real behavior change. However, real change is possible if we remain determined and willing to observe the specific ways in which we self-sabotage by believing in false ideas. We are all capable of change once we learn to stop self-torture and find meaningful reasons to change. The drive to change must come from the heart, and it begins with radical self-acceptance. When efforts at behavior change fail, it is usually because the intent to change comes from the thinking mind instead of a heartfelt desire to change.

Self-Numbing Creates a Living Death

To accomplish something unique and meaningful in life, we need to surrender the self-identity's investment in emotional numbing. This numbing deadens our creativity and resourcefulness. Emotional numbing or deadening is so pervasive that it becomes subconscious. However, on our journey to awakening it is important to become aware of all the ways we self-numb.

SUGGESTED PRACTICE

Take a moment to reflect on your own preferred methods of self-numbing. Then, ask yourself these questions:

1. *How often do you deliberately go numb?*
2. *What is the upside of this numbing?*
3. *What is the downside?*
4. *How does being numb feel in your body?*
5. *What happens to your mind when you go numb?*

To let go of the deadness we feel when we self-numb, we need to value being awake and alive. When we are fully present for our own life, we inevitably have a positive effect on everyone in our world. Most of us do not value knowing our real feelings, bodily sensations, and clear perceptions. However, we are fully capable of a much richer, more authentic, present and accounted-for life. Knowing and accepting our experience just as it is, we learn the value of what it means to be a human being. Our goal is to be simply and thoroughly human.

Nothing Special

Our individual self-identities are largely the same in structure and function as all others. Only the content varies from person to person. However, the content of our self-identity is insignificant. Either we all are special, or no one is. We all inherently know this, and yet we invest a lot of energy in trying to be better than or more special than or the favored one. We are all equally special or equally not special. Striving to be otherwise is futile in terms of the truth of what is so. Those people who believe we are special think we are special just the way we already are.

What is special about us is shared by everyone equally. Namely, we are children created in the image of God. Given to us freely, our divine lineage is neither earned nor deserved. It is our birthright as human beings. The remarkable gift we have is the ability to realize our oneness with the presence of God in all things. We can fully realize this truth through correct teaching, determined effort and divine grace freely bestowed.

Simply Human Is Good Enough

We need to affirm our inherent self-nature. All the spiritual practices in the world amount to nothing until we recognize and accept who we are.

The idea of giving up all our self-improvement projects is counterintuitive. While we do have to surrender seeking to find, we must seek first before surrendering. We seek until the seeking gives itself up. Our own efforts will not suffice. We do not find by seeking, but we must seek wholeheartedly, with our entire mind, body and spirit until the seeking gives itself up without any deliberate effort on our part.

You do not find without seeking, nor do you find by seeking. Paradox is evident in every aspect of this path. Passionately seeking for the truth of your being is absolutely required, but never enough. You cannot force the hand of God. It is possible and necessary to go very far down the spiritual path by your own efforts, especially when guided by a competent teacher and a correct understanding of how to practice. Hard work and determined effort definitely pay off and lead to a more enjoyable life that is less toxic to everyone. Yet the final step is always taken by God. We cannot do it by our self. Our own ego or self-identity will never surrender at the required depth.

In John 6:60, Jesus' disciples react to the enormity of his teachings: *On hearing it, many of his disciples said, 'This is a hard teaching. Who can accept it?* Yes, it is a hard teaching, hard to express and even harder to understand and follow. Throughout his teaching, Jesus speaks indirectly, metaphorically. It is only towards the end of his life that he says to his disciples, *Though I have been speaking figuratively, a time is coming when I will no longer use this kind of language but will tell you plainly about my Father* (John 16:25).

Can we speak plainly, simply, about our truth? Can we tell our truth just as it is, without elaboration, justification, or even explanation? Can we be who we are, nothing more, nothing less? When we cease making everything complicated, the Truth is revealed just as it is: simple, direct, and radiant. *Our form now being no-form, in going and returning, we never leave home* (*Daily Chants and Recitations*, 2005, p. 35). Standing straight, seeing clearly, we can enter the Kingdom of Heaven now.

Whose Mind Is It?

> *Using the mind to look for reality is delusion.*
> *Not using the mind to look for reality is awareness.*
> *Freeing oneself from words is liberation.*
>
> Bodhidharma (Pine, R., 1989, p. 49)

If there is only one Mind, who then is asking questions? Who is answering? The conventional, reflexive answer will leave us stuck in the cement we continuously pour around our self. We will struggle to break free of conditioned, automatic thinking that is not thinking, but ruminating, obsessing, fantasizing and worrying.

There are not two minds, one awake and one asleep. There is only Mind just as it is, nothing more, nothing less. This Mind does not wake up and does not go to sleep.

Yet questions arise. The best questions are those that speak of a very personal struggle and a deep need to know. These questions will often arise from the thinking mind, which is not a problem, if they are also heartfelt and personal. However, questions of a more curious, impersonal, or intellectual nature are of little benefit to anyone and will be deflected or ignored by a skilled teacher.

In a group setting, questions that are meaningful to one person will inevitably resonate with others as well. Thus, all can benefit as this questioning process helps to elicit spiritual wisdom from the one Mind of the teacher and the group members. At the same time, questions whose answers can be found by an internet search are not helpful and depress the energy and consciousness of the group. Part of the art of effective teaching is to learn to quickly deter such questions and refocus on the underlying truth and awareness of our total being and shared presence.

At its best, a deep questioning together can prompt an awakening in one who is completely present and absorbed. While rare, these spontaneous experiences can occur anywhere and everywhere, even while talking to a spiritual teacher! Wherever and however this profound shift in consciousness occurs, it always appears to emerge spontaneously in one with a passionate need to know who has surrendered to a deep internal stillness.

First Awakening

Albert Low in his book *Hakuin on Kensho* (2006, p. 12) describes kensho or a first genuine awakening: *Kensho is not an experience. With kensho, the way we experience is changed fundamentally.* This is an excellent description from a highly experienced teacher of a very difficult to describe process.

An initial awakening is powerful and life altering, yet also embryonic. The person's life is forever changed. There can no longer be any doubt about the truth of the teachings. Buddhists know these teachings about Truth as the *Dharma*. Yet, until the new way of knowing has been extensively integrated and explored, and automatic, conditioned beliefs and behaviors released, much more work is required.

Once we know experientially for ourselves what is real, we find it possible to have real faith, not a series of concepts that we have decided to believe. The aspiration in us to awaken deeply for the benefit of all sentient beings including our self grows ever stronger. An awareness of the inner connectedness of all beings emerges. Each step of the spiritual journey involves the progressive relinquishing of the sense of being separate or special, or of being anything at all except an ordinary human being.

Zen Masters have many ways of testing a student's depth of realization. For a real awakening to have occurred, a clear description of an experience of nondual awareness is not enough. Nor is it sufficient to report an event in the past, no matter how dramatic or intriguing. There must also be an ability to demonstrate behaviorally the understanding in the moment, right now, on demand, in front of the teacher. *Let's see what you've got!* might be the teacher's injunction; or *Show me this new understanding!* A largely conceptual grasp of nonduality is of limited use. It is necessary to deepen this intuitive realization until we manifest it continuously in our behavior.

An experience or glimpse of nondual reality is invaluable. To be truly useful, however, the awakening must become not just an isolated experience, but an ongoing reality that shapes and alters every experience of our life. The nondual awareness must become who we are, moment to moment.

Embodiment

Even the deepest awakening needs integration into ordinary life, and this integration process continues for many years afterward. In some ways, having a mature teacher who personally has traversed this path is even more valuable after awakening than before.

An essential aspect of this integration is embodiment. Awakening is an experiential transformation that involves the total being. Nothing is omitted. The new awareness is all encompassing, including the emotions, thinking processes, and the body at a deeply biological level. The integration of this new awareness continues for the remainder of this lifetime. From my perspective, the full embodiment of awakened awareness is never finished. We are all works in progress. Living out the awareness completely in every moment is the work that remains after even the deepest of spiritual awakenings.

With continued practice of the sort I have described in this book, we will notice real changes in ourselves. We will lose interest in argument as we come to realize that our deeply conditioned, programmed beliefs are not any better than anyone else's. As we lose interest in insisting that our way is God's way, the endless tumult of mental chatter in our head begins to subside. Why should we be right and everyone else wrong? This is an obvious question yet one we rarely ask ourselves. There's a gradual loss of interest in meaningless activities. As a result, our lives become quieter and more peaceful. We become better friends, lovers, and companions as we progressively lose interest in needing to always be right. Although I experienced several profound shifts in consciousness previously, including kensho, it was only after the abiding awakening in 2002 that I lost all interest in being right. What a relief!

There may be blissful moments as well from time to time. However, there is no effort to create or hang onto anything at all, including bliss. Bliss is nice, and it comes and goes on its own, as do all other possible human experiences. Everything is accepted, recognized for what it is, and allowed to move on when the time is right. The natural state of awakened awareness is internal stillness, quiet contentment and peacefulness, holding onto nothing and pushing nothing away.

Almost every experience in life can be enjoyable. If we are not enjoying an experience, it will serve us well to at least try to be curious about the lack of pleasure we are experiencing. Can we be one with the experience as it is and try not to judge it? Is it ok for an experience to be what it is and not some other experience? If not, why not? Of course, the same is true for people. Can we simply allow them to be who and what they are without needing or wanting them to be different? Can we do the same with our self?

In my life I have found living in upstate New York to be a challenge because of the winters. Having grown up in the South, I find the long, cold, dark season of winter in the northeast very difficult to accept. Dealing with dark, cold weather that seems to last forever without judging it is a challenge for me. My mind would prefer something else entirely. Being aware of the weather conditions is not the issue for me but choosing to dislike the weather on a given winter day and wishing it were different is.

We create needless stress for ourselves when we react negatively and judgmentally to a given experience. The stress is not the result of the experience itself. We need to notice with tolerance, acceptance and curiosity our internal reactions. All challenges will not disappear with awakening. As human beings, we will always have challenges, issues and problems will arise as long as we live. However, with continued embodiment of the awakened awareness, we will feel a tremendous lightness of being that allows us to experience our challenges with less stress, and sometimes even with humor.

As our mind becomes quieter on its own, we will notice that we do not feel miserable as often as before, if we indeed feel it at all. We recognize that feeling miserable is self-created, and not caused by or dependent on external events. This is a huge realization. Other people are not the cause of my suffering! Imagine that! As we lose interest in comparing what is with what should be but is not, we gradually decrease how often we make ourselves miserable.

Contentment becomes the default setting, even when life events occasionally intrude. Applying objective, curious awareness to these disruptions reveals remaining areas in our body and mind where conditioned, programmed beliefs still hold sway. Continual deprogramming of any automatic, unconscious beliefs is all that is required to free us from being chained to our self-identity and its endless cycles of craving and aversion. These automatic beliefs are hard to release until we become aware of them. As such, we learn to welcome the emergence of unreleased, undigested old feelings, patterns of behavior and mistaken assumptions. Once a previously unconscious mistaken belief has emerged into awareness, it can be deconstructed.

Deepening the New Understanding

The inevitable next step is to deepen and solidify our grasp of this true reality. Continuous dwelling in awareness can be somewhat elusive, but with continued deprogramming of unconscious beliefs, feelings, patterns of behavior and assumptions, it becomes normal to live routinely in the awareness of what is. It becomes increasingly easier to refrain from relapsing into automatic conditioned beliefs.

Watching deeply ingrained, heavily programmed thinking emerge repeatedly is very beneficial. This self-observation makes the connection between our beliefs and the physical and emotional reactions in our body clear. It is useful to practice moving into the role of watcher or observer whenever a thought or belief has triggered some internal reaction in us. We might think, *I have a little attachment there. I'm starting to believe my thoughts are real. I'm beginning to take them seriously.*

Whenever I take my programmed thoughts and beliefs seriously, the inevitable result is discomfort or even suffering. I will make myself miserable in some way because of believing my thoughts. Therefore, I try to watch the thinking process instead of identifying with it. Normally we have a thought, and immediately identify with it. We believe the thought is our thought and that our thoughts are real and important. In awakening, we learn that is not the case. In an important but difficult to understand way, our thoughts are no more ours than the clouds drifting by are ours. Thoughts, like clouds, are simply occurrences in the vast field of awareness. They normally do not need to be taken seriously.

We all have individual, conditioned beliefs about who we are. We normally believe in a me that is consistent and continuous in time and space. These are just conditioned beliefs. When we clear the smoke of that conditioning, only Mind remains. We need to bring this radical shift in awareness fully into our day to day life. If the awakening is real, it will transform our daily life. This process of integration will continue indefinitely.

There may well be individuals who completely transcend being a human being. I have never met one, so I cannot say for sure. The rest of us most likely will not transcend the human state, and as such we must always keep working on integrating whatever awakening we have had. We must remain humble and realistic. We must strive to never knowingly hurt others, for if we do, we have reverted to dualistic thinking and a sense of separation. We must not abandon the awareness of what is ultimately real. This is everyone's natural state, and this is where we already are when we are not actively distracting and confusing ourselves.

Zen Buddhism puts constant emphasis on polishing the mind. In contemporary psychological language we call it working through. No matter how deep the awakening is, we're still living in a human body, and we still have internal conditioning to notice and to try to free ourselves from. This process continues to be true until we physically die. We must take responsibility for our actions and pay attention to the results.

Limitless Awareness

The awareness we are describing includes but is not contained by time, space and causality. No effort on our part can create it. It emerges spontaneously from no-mind.

Until we have a deep personal experience of the truth, others who have explored this unfamiliar terrain will be helpful in guiding us. This is where faith as we normally understand it becomes important. The primary article of faith that's helpful is to have some level of belief that awakening is possible for us in this lifetime. Others who are in no way different from us have awakened to their true nature. Some of these people dwell in a continuous awareness of the presence of God. Let this be our goal.

This realization is about who we already are and always have been. To know this truth deeply is transforming. The experience is about an internal perceptual shift to an awareness that everything is of the same nature and yet also radically different.

The first experience of awareness is usually transitory but can become our permanent state with further practice and grace. What's required is to die to everything we currently believe is real. Although this sounds frightening to the ego, dying in this way is the path of liberation. The only thing that dies is our mistaken beliefs about reality and the false sense of who we are. You will not lose anything you would want to have back!

When gain and loss no longer apply to us, we know our original face before our parents were born. Receiving grace depends on our willingness to give up who and what we think we are. Grace is eternal, omnipresent and always freely given. Are we open to receiving this gift of grace? God's grace is everywhere all the time. I wake up every morning and say, *Thy will be done. I have no will of my own. I surrender myself totally to you. Direct me and use me as you wish.*

Chapter Seven

DOING WITHOUT A DOER

The further one goes, / The less one knows. / For this reason, / The sage knows without journeying / understands without looking, / accomplishes without acting.

Mair, V. H., *Tao Te Ching*, 1998

In *The Hollow Men*, T.S. Eliot (1980, p. 56) vividly describes the almost imperceptible buffer between our direct, unmediated experience and the dry, brittle reality that we mistakenly accept as all we can know:

> *Between the idea*
> *And the reality*
> *Between the motion*
> *And the act*
> *Falls the Shadow*

We are capable of much richer and more colorful experiences than we believe possible. Opening our eyes to truth is like suddenly being able to see in color after a lifetime of seeing only shades of black and white.

I first confronted the stark world Eliot portrays when I was a college student. Lines from *The Hollow Men* sank deeply into my curious mind and refused to let go. Eliot accurately depicts the monotony and tedium of normal life, which ends *not with a bang, but a whimper* (Eliot, Op. cit.). We normally live our lives in shades of gray, timid and frightened. It often appears that our primary goal is to reduce risk and uncertainty. Our continuous efforts to maintain at least the illusion of control creates constriction, impairing creative and spontaneous action. We have lost sight of our birthright of freedom, direct action and intuitive knowing.

Wu Wei

The Chinese term *wu wei* refers to action that occurs without conscious intent or planning. It occurs of its own and is powerful and direct. The awakened mind is completely still, even when the body is moving. Out of this profound stillness arises action that's pure, unpremeditated, and skillful. It is stillness in action or Mind moving freely through the world of form. Think of a samurai who is a master swordsman. When it is time to strike, the sword moves with explosive speed and force. It seems to have a life of its own. The same effect can be achieved by one who is highly skilled with any tool. Professional musicians experience their instrument as an extension of themselves. It takes years of training to be able to experience a sense of oneness with a tool or instrument. The best artists use their paintbrush in the same manner as the samurai uses his sword. When everything is working perfectly, the brush seems to have a life of its own.

In Christian terms, this spontaneous action is the result of total surrender of the individual will to the will of God. This complete giving up of my own will allows the Holy Spirit to activate the body-mind in whatever way it chooses. In Buddhist terminology, such free, direct, and skillful action is Right Action. This phrase refers to action in the world that arises out of no-mind awareness.

The Buddhist scriptures or sutras tell us to move without moving, to travel without traveling, to see without seeing, to laugh without laughing, to hear without hearing, to know without knowing, to be happy without being happy, to walk without walking, to stand without standing. When we live our life in this way, we are one with the Great Way. Life unfolds of its own with minimal resistance.

Not Two

Form and emptiness are not two. However, not being different does not mean they are the same. In our ordinary day-to-day life, we perceive differences without simultaneously perceiving the underlying sameness. Awakening is the experiential awareness of the unity that underlies all perceived differences. At the same time, in clear awareness there is no denial of differentiation. For example, tulips are not the same as daisies, humans are not the same as an oak tree, etc. The world of form is neither separate from nor identical to the world of emptiness. Ultimately, all differences are based on perception.

The manifestation of formlessness in the world is doing without a doer, acting without an actor, thinking without a thinker. A total or nearly total integration represents the thorough interpenetration of form and emptiness. In Christian language, the Father and the Son aren't two, nor even one. Yet, simultaneously, they are also separate and distinct.

To understand this noncognitive realization, we need to understand accurately the meaning of emptiness or nothingness. Emptiness in this context is not empty; nothingness is not nothing. This strange emptiness is full, although we cannot define of what it is full.

Nothing we try to say about this fullness will be quite accurate. Analogous to a pluripotent stem cell that can become any cell in the body, this fullness is infinite potentiality.

Spiritual experiences can have various degrees of depth. Even a brief, yet direct glimpse of emptiness is profound. Suchness is the formless, indefinable substance that composes the universe and is impossible to describe. In experiencing suchness, we realize that emptiness is not empty but full. Suchness is infinite potentiality that can take the appearance of all forms. We can know this intuitively and experientially to be true.

Because of our conditioning and its distortions, we misperceive this substance-less something. We perceive forms to be solid and enduring because of our conditioning and its related perceptual distortions. In one way, forms are indeed solid and enduring. For example, our coffee maker will be on the counter waiting for us every morning. However, in perceiving the form or solid aspect of the world, we forget that the form is only a part of the whole. The non-form aspect is equally real and important. To know the world of form is to be aware of differentiation of all kinds. If we only perceive the world of form, we perpetuate stress and its related misery and suffering in our lives. On the other hand, to grasp only the nondual nature of Reality leaves us nonfunctional in terms of coping with the ordinary world. We must integrate thoroughly the experiential knowing of nonduality into the duality necessary to function in daily life.

The most effective way for this integration to occur is to become aware of spontaneous no-mind behavior that has no mediation by our self-identity. While we have all had multiple experiences of this sort, we usually do not notice or remember these no-mind experiences. This is primarily because of our dualistic way of perceiving. When we act freely and directly out of no-mind, the thinking mind is off-line. This is because behavior from no-mind occurs outside of space and time, so there is often little to no memory trace. We are not taught or encouraged to pay attention to such occurrences. However, the more we learn to recognize them, the more they will occur.

In John 3:6, Jesus describes to Nicodemus the freedom experienced by those who have disappeared to their self-identity. For such a person action arises from no-self.

> *You should not be surprised at my saying, 'You must be born again.' The wind blows wherever it pleases. You hear its sound, but you cannot tell where it comes from or where it is going. So it is of everyone born of the spirit.*

As we reflect on the descriptions of the characteristics of truly free behavior in this passage from the Gospel of John, we need to allow ourselves to remember our own similar experiences. We will find that as we remember these experiences, we will also remember the feeling of freedom that accompanied them. This is real freedom, not self-centered ego-based freedom.

Behavior from No-Mind

No-Mind behavior is free, effortless, and inherently enjoyable no matter what we're doing. As such, all activity is equally enjoyable. Only our thinking mind can prevent us from equally enjoying all activities, for the thinking mind will automatically judge, compare and evaluate. This process of judging, comparing and preferring removes us from our own direct experience.

In an absolute sense, nothing is good or bad, right or wrong, better or worse. We need to notice any tendency in our thinking mind as we read these words to want to disagree, dismiss, or edit. This thinking and judging function is how we separate ourselves from our own direct, intuitive knowing.

Behavior that occurs from no-mind awareness allows us to have an experience that is direct, spontaneous, unpremeditated, and unpredictable; as though the behavior occurs on its own. We aren't guiding or directing it. Such free and direct behavior has power and effectiveness in the world. One reason for this power is that free action bypasses the opposition or resistance of others. Additionally, there's no personal credit or blame for actions occurring out of no-mind awareness. There's an ongoing recognition that it wasn't us who took an action. The nature of the self-identity or thinking mind, on the other hand, is to continually monitor, assess, judge, and evaluate everything said and done. No-mind awareness results in behavior that frees us from this continuous, obsessive, fear-based self-monitoring.

There is no need to second-guess the impact of behavior that arises from no-self. The self-identity always will insist that we should doubt ourselves. Our goal with the self-identity is to accept it as it is but not believe it's who we are. It is only one aspect of who we are. The self-identity is always with us in this life. In accepting it, but not completely identifying with it, we set ourselves free from its grasp.

We need to observe the fears and worries of the ego without taking them seriously. Ongoing faith, practice, and devotion will allow us to see this truth in all of life's circumstances.

The behavior occurring out of no-mind is minimally tiring and often highly energizing. We tend to lose interest in and forget the meaningless trivia of life when dwelling in no-mind awareness. We forget so much of what our minds obsessed over before the experience of this awareness, so much so that it may appear as though there's short-term memory impairment. As we continue to dwell in the present moment and lose interest in the obsessive ruminations of our mind, we lose interest in compulsively reminding ourselves of the trivia of daily existence. We no longer have any need to rehearse in our mind all the perceived slights and mistreatments we imagine we've received. This meaningless and trivial mental content will slowly disappear as we continue to lose interest in it, leaving us more able to process reality and let go of the deeply unsatisfying fantasy world we construct in our mind.

Experience that arises from no-mind has a timeless quality. In this no-mind awareness, there continues to be an ability to function in a world controlled by time-consciousness, while simultaneously remaining aware of the arbitrary nature of time. The concept of time passing is limited to the world of the ego. Past and future only exist as we create them in our minds. The ability to plan as needed is not impaired, but the difference is that we can make plans without worrying about an imaginary future.

There's a loss of interest in constructing causal explanations. Interest in *why* questions disappears. In other words, we lose interest in our own drama, and eventually see our personal dramas as boring and tedious instead of fascinating and important. Behavior from this no-mind awareness just flows. The inner experience is observing our own behavior with a mixture of curiosity and mild bemusement. We don't know what we'll do or say until we observe ourselves in action. Trust and surrender are the key issues in remaining present and allowing this spontaneous unfolding to occur.

True Nature in Action

Such direct, powerful, unpremeditated behavior is a clear marker for presence awareness acting freely in the world. It is our true nature in action. While T.S. Eliot does a beautiful job describing the stale and brittle ordinary state, we find a remarkable description of freedom in action in the poetry of the tenth ox-herding picture.

These pictures and accompanying descriptions represent the stages of spiritual insight. Originally a Taoist story, they were revised and updated by a twelfth century Chinese monk Guo-an Shi-yuan. Numerous subsequent versions exist. We will refer to the version found in Roshi Philip Kapleau's seminal book *The Three Pillars of Zen* (1980, p. 323).

> *Barechested, barefooted, he comes into the marketplace.*
> *Muddied and dust covered, how broadly he grins!*

Without recourse to mystic powers,
Withered trees he swiftly brings to bloom.

This man is truly free to be himself, exactly as he is. He has no concern for how others perceive him. He may or may not follow social rules and conventions. In every moment his behavior is in accord with the will of God and is guided by the Holy Spirit. He represents the authenticity and spontaneity of a fully embodied enlightenment. There is no gap between thought and action. His moment-to-moment life is a full explication of the Buddhist dharma, or truth. There is nothing more to develop or accomplish. All of his questions have vanished and cannot be found anywhere, even in a memory.

> *SUGGESTED PRACTICE*
>
> *Take a few minutes to reflect on your own experiences. Allow yourself some time now to remember experiences from the past in your life that had some of these no-mind behavior qualities such as feeling free, unencumbered, and spontaneous. Then, reflect on experiences of unselfconscious behavior you have had in your life. Recall your feelings during the experience and ask yourself these questions:*
>
> *1. Were you worried about anything?*
> *2. Were you obsessing or ruminating?*
> *3. Were your actions skillful in a seemingly effortless manner?*
> *4. Would you like to be this way more of the time? Most of the time?*
>
> *This is your birthright. You can reclaim it now.*

The Feeling of Awareness

Given this understanding of the behavioral manifestation of awakening, it becomes clear why forcing ourselves to conform to some code of behavior that seems unnatural couldn't possibly help to facilitate it. In the spiritual search it is best to trust our own deep-seated instincts instead of our conditioned, self-centered desires and wishes.

Learning to listen to and respect what we intuitively know to be true is an important step on this path. How we feel emotionally and physically is often a very good indicator of whether a path or behavior is in our best interest. In no-mind behavior, our best interests are in complete accord with the best interests of all. We must learn to listen to and trust the wisdom of our heart and our body. If it feels constricting and life-denying, it probably is. If it feels free, liberating, opening, and accepting, it probably is.

Choosing life-affirming actions and losing interest in convictions and beliefs liberates us from self-induced suffering. Remember, this path is about disappearing as a constructed, historic being. We do not become intellectually thick or stupid. We do not need to forget everything learned in a lifetime of personal growth and effort. Acquired knowledge is not erased and judgment is not impaired. We'll still know how to drive a car and feed our children. The cause of our suffering is not the information we have acquired about the world. Rather, it is the recognition that we create suffering by our belief in conditioned, automatic assumptions that are limited, untrue, and flawed.

Learn to listen to and trust direct, intuitive knowing. We will only occasionally find advice from others helpful. Almost everything we hear from others, no matter how well intentioned, is merely an expression of their own ego-based fears and desires.

No one who has experienced it would ever imply that a true path is easy, but we need to have the courage to take the first step on that path and the courage to persevere in the face of obstacles and opposition. We need to realize that our efforts are not only for ourselves, but also for the benefit of all beings. In the deepest awareness, we realize that we are not separate from others.

Discernment

We need to ask for guidance in discerning God's will for us. It is essential that we seek this guidance with absolute humility and willingness to be shown the way. This willingness to be shown and to follow through with right action is the meaning of surrender. There may be times when we will recognize an action should be taken that is not appealing or even goes against our own best judgement. In these cases, it is okay to wait for further discernment. If that discernment continues to reveal a need for us to take that action, it is probably wise to follow through on the action that is being suggested. This process does not negate the thinking mind or undercut the role of reason or critical judgement in the usual sense. If we remain willing to receive guidance from the no-mind, we will be able to recognize what is being revealed. This process helps us to develop effective and skillful discernment.

No-mind is our friend. Not knowing is our friend. We need to adopt the perspective of not knowing and learn to be ok with uncertainty. It is a myth that we should know what we are doing all the time. A closed mind knows programming and belief, not revealed truth. No-mind knows revealed truth. We must remain open and be willing to dwell frequently in uncertainty to know revealed truth. Learning to tolerate this uncertainty is a large part of the spiritual path as we continue seeking to know God's will for us in our lives. We need to engage in this searching from a place of watchful waiting rather than a place of doubt or anxiety. We do not need to expend effort in trying to achieve a particular outcome. This waiting for guidance to be revealed is actively passive, open, curious, and receptive.

It is highly beneficial to develop a profound tolerance and embrace of uncertainty. In the 14th century spiritual classic *The Cloud of Unknowing (1996)* p. 53, the unknown author states:

When I speak of "darkness", I mean the, absence of knowledge. If you are unable to understand something or if you have forgotten it, are you not in the dark as regards this thing? You cannot see it with your mind's eye. Well, in the same way, I have not said "cloud" but cloud of unknowing. For it is a darkness of unknowing that lies between you and your God.

It is not always easy or clear to discern the difference between what our conditioned mind wants and what God wants. To recognize it requires us to trust, use our intuition and surrender. We will find that God's will tends to be insistent. Repeatedly revisiting in our mind an idea or plan of action is often a clear sign that we are receiving Divine guidance to follow through on that plan of action.

We need to stay present and attuned, always open to further guidance. Recognizing and carrying out guidance skillfully requires understanding and practice. These skills develop over time. It will be helpful for us to remember experiences where we felt guided in the past and review how things evolved. We will see that typically things went well, and often much better than we could ever imagine. We may feel anxiety about committing to a course of action, but we often notice a feeling of relief afterwards. We need to try to maintain awareness of the entire process. It is inherent in all of us to be able to do so.

Eventually this other way of knowing becomes second nature and is mostly effortless. Interruptions in the flow of awareness come as conditioned beliefs and habits are triggered. This eruption of conditioning and fear is not a problem. Rather, it is an opportunity to become more aware of unconscious programming and release it. In other words, it is an opportunity to become free. Everything that appears to be a problem will yield to a calm and present awareness.

Chapter Eight

DAILY LIFE IS THE WAY

*Not only here, not only there,
Truth's right before your very eyes.*

Affirming Faith in Mind

We are already whole and complete. We already have everything we need. Our life does not need to be different in any way. There is no past or future except what our minds create. This present moment is the only time we have. We need to make the most of it!

To awaken during this lifetime, we do not need a better or different mind or body. It's not necessary to stop smoking, lose weight, get in shape, become a vegetarian, abstain from sex, give up drinking, or perform rituals of any kind to experience full awakening. We do not need to subscribe to any beliefs or practices. All our perceived burdens, hassles, and overwhelming responsibilities can be wonderful gifts. All perceived obstacles are fictitious. Any responsibilities we currently have are priceless encouragements to continue the path to direct truth.

We need to stay focused and let nothing dissuade us. The normal issues of daily life are the stuff of which awakening is made. We need to look to our own lives to show us the way. The truth is, we must come to our own realization of what is so, and we can.

We need to trust in our own deepest knowing. This direct awareness has always been with us. We cannot lose it or gain it. It is ever present.

When we lose all interest in near and far, then past and future are no more. With every thought and every spoken word, we separate ourselves from the primal source, and as such forget our true home in this real world.

Forget Past and Future

We worry about an imaginary future that will never happen, that exists nowhere but in our imagination. We live an *as if* life in our self-created *as if* world, and as such we worry about events that might take place in the future as if they were happening in the present moment. Our bodies and our unconscious minds can't distinguish the difference between constructed fantasies and reality.

Reality is our friend. We need to make peace with it and relax into what's real for us in the present moment. We need to allow our present experience to be just as it is, without judgment or qualification. In so doing, we may notice internal resistance to acceptance of what is. However, the more we become aware of our internal resistance to accepting what is real, the less rigid and stuck we become.

We delude ourselves into believing that it is somehow beneficial for us to construct terrifying scenarios of imaginary futures in our minds and react to these constructed daydreams as if they're real. We cannot know the future, meaning there is a very good possibility we are worrying about something that will never materialize. We believe a story we have made up in our mind. This is the first step in creating conflict with each other and within ourselves.

The Ego's Job Description

The self-identity or ego is the historic, constructed version of who we think we are. However, it's not all we are. The ego's job is to pretend that it can control events in life, but that is an illusion. The ego cannot control events. Period. We tend to buy into this illusion and as such believe we can and should control future events. We cannot. This one erroneous belief is the source of endless, needless, mental suffering for us. We habitually worry because we fear we will fail in predicting future events, and even more, we feel it is our responsibility to worry. If we let go of this false belief, we simultaneously are relieved of any worry.

In addition to holding the erroneous belief that we are responsible for predicting future events, we believe we are responsible for preventing undesired future events as well. If we do not succeed at this impossible project, we judge ourselves harshly. We believe this self-judgment is deserved because we erroneously believe that we could have successfully prevented the undesired outcome if only we had tried harder. We have deceived ourselves into believing that if we worry and obsess enough, we can prevent unwanted experiences from happening in the future. The only result this kind of thinking can produce is chronic fear and anxiety.

True thinking and planning are useful and necessary, but it is important to be able to discern the difference between productive thinking and obsessive worry. We can differentiate between the two by noticing the emotional tone of the thoughts in our mind. Actual thinking and useful planning usually carry no emotional tone, whereas worry and fearful obsessing have a very negative, unpleasant emotional tone. True thinking and planning result in real accomplishments. Worry only results in more worry, anxiety, energetic depletion and fearful thoughts and feelings.

Should We Remember the Past?

Objective review of the past can be useful when done correctly. There is a reason psychotherapy is often very beneficial. We need to notice if our self-reflection is helpful to us. This is true whether we are speaking with another person or turning inward by ourselves. Do we feel better for doing it? Does our self-reflection seem to liberate energy? Do we feel more hopeful and optimistic? Do we feel less stuck in some important area of our life? Do new ways of conceptualizing a problem occur that create opportunities for action and behavior change? These are the results of healthy, productive self-reflection.

Our memories of past events are always current constructions. We can never remember precisely what happened in the past. Our normal memory is a self-serving re-creation of a fragment or a sliver of a moment in time. Many fascinating psychological experiments demonstrate the constructed and pliable nature of memory.

Even so, there can be real benefits to a productive review of past events in our lives. In psychological research literature, there is ample evidence of the value of various approaches to relieving emotional stress. When people who are suffering tell their personal story to another human being who can be present for that conversation, multiple benefits can spontaneously arise.

Simply writing down our experience without sharing it with anyone has been demonstrated to have enormous healing potential (Pennebaker, J., and Evans, J., 2014). The lingering effects of traumatic events can often be mitigated by putting our experience into a coherent narrative. This is one reason why police will often have victims tell their story repeatedly. With each repetition to a calm and supportive audience, the narrative will become more coherent with fewer dissociative events, disruptions, forgetting, and emotional intrusions.

The presence of another person who is interested, empathic, attentive, open, and accepting can be very healing. My graduate training program in clinical psychology leaned heavily towards behavioral interventions. I, however, found the empathic listening advocated by Carl Rogers to be enormously helpful to clients and more in tune with my own natural manner of relating. A competent psychotherapist is trained to do this very thing. A friend or relative who is a naturally gifted listener is invaluable. For a contemporary version of Roger's method see Eugene Gendlin's book in the bibliography.

Guilt

It has been my personal experience that there is little if any benefit from feeling guilty or ashamed over some real or imagined failing. Feelings of guilt do not energize or help us to recognize creative solutions to seemingly unsolvable problems, nor do they enable us to act more effectively in the world. However, there is also tremendous value in an honest recognition of times where we have been insensitive, clumsy or harmful to others. It is important to take responsibility for our unskillful behavior and make amends. Enormous benefit can occur from acknowledging our mistakes, offering a genuine apology and seeking forgiveness when appropriate. Seven of the twelve steps of Alcoholics Anonymous focus on this process and can be beneficial to anyone.

Most of us, however, are plagued by conscious and unconscious guilt that needlessly restricts our freedom. It is important to carefully evaluate the sources of guilt in our life. It is possible to use guilt somewhat effectively to improve behavior, but I do not see this happen very often. What are the underlying beliefs and assumptions that create the experience of guilt? The constructed, historic self-identity creates the experience of guilt. Guilt arises when we create a fantasy of the past. This fantasy must involve the belief that we could have and should have acted in some way other than how we did act. The events in our life happened exactly the way they did. It is a mistaken belief to assume that events could have or should have happened differently. It can help us release traumatic memories to recognize that nothing in the past could or should have been different, including us.

I am not saying everything happens for a reason, because I do not know if that idea is true. I do know there are an infinite number of ways of perceiving and interpreting an event, and we can often change our experience by perceiving an experience in a different manner. In addition, there will often be a recognition after the fact of some benefit accruing from experiences that were painful and disappointing at the time. Torturing ourselves over fantasies of how badly we performed in the past rarely improves our current behavior and is often self-indulgent and without value. Guilt, like pride and many other normal human emotions, can be narcissistic and self-absorbed. Any time we rehash or create an imaginary past, we're not present for our life now. Being present in our real life should be our goal. Losing ourselves in fantasies of the past and future is not recommended.

If we have behaved badly in an objective sense, and others agree with this self-assessment, it is beneficial to resolve to change our behavior. Self-flagellation, however, rarely leads to constructive behavior change. An essential part of the waking-up process is to refuse to indulge in fruitless activities that reinforce fears and desires. The fulfillment of our heavily programmed desires will do nothing but distract us from the true source of satisfaction, which is the direct, conscious, phenomenal experience of our moment-to-moment existence.

As human beings, we are biological animals with basic needs for survival, clothing, food, and shelter. We also have ordinary needs for affection, companionship, sex, nurturance, rest, relaxation, and financial security. Being assertive in a healthy way to meet these legitimate, universal human needs doesn't interfere with spiritual awakening. Acting like a responsible adult is a good thing. Taking reasonable care of others for whom we're responsible and of ourselves is wisdom in action. The Self doesn't second-guess common sense choices and responsible adult behavior. However, the conditioned mind creates problems. From the perspective of the Self, problems don't exist. If we learn to pay attention to our internal physical and emotional signals, we will find guidance in the right direction, especially if we ignore the conditioned mind's thoughts and beliefs.

On reflection, we will see that questioning our own judgment creates nothing but guilt and worry. The unfortunate result is often to act out of conditioned thought instead of instinct and intuition. These distinctions can seem very subtle to the thinking, conditioned mind. The real solution to these issues is to learn to see clearly through awakening to what is. Then all important questions will be answered, and the unimportant questions will disappear.

Intimacy

True intimacy with all that is comes from the loss of interest in self-protection and striving. If we begin to experience self-centered fears, we need to simply notice and accept them. As we move closer to full awakening, we will discover that negative, painful feelings arise because we have relapsed into old habits of believing the fears and self-absorption of the conditioned mind. This is exactly how we make our lives miserable.

Intimacy with others is only possible if we accept them as they are without trying to change them in any way. This total acceptance happens naturally of its own when we are present, open and not lost in our own thoughts and opinions.

SUGGESTED PRACTICE

Notice your interactions with people over the next week. Let yourself become aware of how much time and energy you spend critically

> *judging and attempting to change others. Notice how completely fruitless these efforts are, and how people will not respond well to your attempts to change them. Do we really know what is best for another person? Can we be certain our way is better for them than their way? The same approach can be applied to our interactions with animals.*

Engaging in this exercise often reveals how incredibly narcissistic our beliefs are. We must give up these useless efforts at changing others. If we do not, real intimacy with anyone will be impossible. We must first have true intimacy with who we are, without judgement, before we can have an intimate relationship with someone else.

Marriage and Family

Unhappy marriages are unhappy for basically the same reason: We want our spouse and loved ones to be present for us without a simultaneous commitment on our part to be present for them. We want to be provided what we do give. If we feel that we are not empathically seen, heard and received by our partner, we feel frustrated, invisible, unimportant or ignored. What we are feeling is a false sense of entitlement. Learn to be fully present for everyone in your life, and all relationships will markedly improve. This does not imply that all relationships are beneficial and should continue. As we learn to be more present for ourselves and others, we will probably recognize some current relationships to not be sustainable. We must be willing to embrace change to grow spiritually.

In wanting the other to be present for us in our misery, we are hoping to receive the one thing that almost no one can give, pure presence. In pure presence, there's no internal dialogue occurring. No judgments are made, and no conclusions drawn. We assign no blame and rarely prescribe a course of action.

Even a moment of pure presence has a profoundly healing and restorative function, especially when we are truly miserable, and the other person is fully present to us. In just such a moment, miracles may occur. One of those miracles might be the temporary cessation of our obsessional, self-absorbed thinking mind. This can and sometimes does happen. Our goal needs to be to learn to calm and soothe ourselves, making us less dependent on others for inner peace and quiet.

Those most exposed to our energy field, such as family, friends, and colleagues, will benefit from changes in us in perceptible ways. This is the real solution to codependency. If we can learn how to calm and soothe ourselves, we let go of the need to change others into our thinking mind's version of who we believe they should be. Relationships usually flounder when we are unsuccessful at manipulating the other person to be a better caregiver. Learning to articulate legitimate needs and wants clearly is highly beneficial to everyone.

Spiritual growth manifests through our behavior in our daily lives. The invaluable insights and realizations that spontaneously arise from our altered awareness benefit everyone. A famous Zen saying is *ordinary mind is the Way*. To paraphrase, an ordinary life is the way.

The ego or self-identity constantly strives to be extraordinary. To end that striving within ourselves, we need to choose to stop viewing ourselves as a self-improvement project. We need to relax into the moment-to-moment awareness of what is, and in turn we will discover how much more satisfying our relationships become. When we cease judging others against an imaginary yardstick in our mind of how they should be, we free ourselves from the ego's control over our judgmental perceptions and beliefs.

> *SUGGESTED PRACTICE*
>
> *Take five minutes twice a day for the next week and reflect on how much time you spend in critical evaluation of yourself and others.*
>
> *Notice how much of the daily content of your mind is repetitive thoughts. Write down these thoughts as you become aware of them. Bring these conditioned thoughts and their underlying beliefs into your full conscious awareness.*
>
> *Do this awareness exercise repeatedly until it becomes clear to you that you're needlessly creating your own suffering. Then, take some time to internalize the following:*
>
> 1. *Harsh judgments of self and others are fruitless.*
> 2. *You can change. Other people can change, but you will never change other people, especially by your disappointment in them or harsh judgment of them.*
> 3. *You will never change your own behavior through self-judgment and castigation.*

Our thinking mind tells us that our beliefs regarding the behavior of others are superior to their beliefs about themselves. We will never change anyone's behavior with feeble and useless attempts at lecturing them about how right we are and how wrong they are. We think our efforts are somewhat heroic, for we may believe we are enlightening the other person regarding changes they should make in themselves. Unfortunately, our efforts to improve others are usually doomed to fail. No matter how noble our efforts to help may seem to us, people rarely change through being lectured, criticized, brow beaten or bullied. This does not mean that there is never a place for judicious, objective, constructive feedback. However, we can often be most helpful by changing ourselves. Part of that change is a change in our perspective of how we see others. Only when we change our internal perspective will we see a resolution to the conflict of trying to teach others what we falsely believe to be a better way of being or doing.

Parenting

In presence awareness, we may do what we reasonably can to assist others in all our relationships. As parents we must educate and teach our children to the best of our ability, while at the same time remembering that our children have their own lives and destiny. Kindness, tolerance, forgiveness, and compassion are always beneficial for self and others. These qualities will emerge more and more frequently in all our relationships, including our role as a parent, as we become increasingly awake and present in the world.

As a psychotherapist, I have seen many difficult parent-child conflicts gradually resolve as one or both parents became more awake and present. In becoming more open, curious, and accepting these parents loosened their tenacious grip on controlling outcomes regarding their children's development. Their children benefitted from this new awareness in their parents in countless ways.

Compassion

True compassion can arise only in a state of pure presence. In this direct awareness of what is, no fundamental separation exists between the object of our compassion and us. Consequently, we do not feel a false sense of duty or obligation to fix the problem the person we are trying to help is experiencing. In pure presence, compassionate behavior arises spontaneously out of the needs of the moment.

The experience of feeling sorry for someone presupposes a separation between us and them that can exist only in the thinking mind. Once we truly understand that we and the other are not two, genuine compassion becomes largely automatic and as natural as breathing. We then understand compassionate behavior to be the direct expression of the Self-operating freely in the world.

Eliminating Compassion Fatigue

When our beliefs of how we should act in each situation no longer control us, compassion fatigue ceases, because we are now listening to our heart, our feelings, and our body instead of our beliefs and convictions.

Reducing the devastating impact of psychological problems in our lives can help enormously to liberate the energy and determination needed to awaken. Two books by Pia Melody have been extremely helpful in reducing codependent thinking in those willing to learn and change. I suggest *Facing Love Addiction* (2003), a book I have read multiple times, which is especially useful to those who suffer with self-sacrifice and self-deprivation. Additionally, she authored another wonderful book which addresses similar concerns entitled, *Facing Codependency* (2003).

Withdrawal and Engagement

Psychotherapy provides the perfect opportunity to demonstrate the enormous benefits and power of presence awareness. There is a universal human need to share our story. We need to feel understood and wish to be accepted and valued despite any trauma we may have experienced. To that end, providing psychological assistance to people in my psychotherapy practice has been deeply rewarding and meaningful. I feel grateful that so many people trusted me to assist them in their personal journey to wholeness.

At the time my personal shift in awareness occurred in 2002, I was seeing as many as fifty individual and couple clients each week.

Immersed in my professional work, I was also helping to raise my younger son and trying to maintain a romantic relationship. I also owned and managed a professional office building where nine other psychotherapists and myself maintained offices. Withdrawing from these important responsibilities was never an option. Apparently, my path has been to maintain full involvement in the world. Yet, for others, their call has been to leave their normal lives, perhaps indefinitely in order to follow their spiritual path.

Sometimes a strategic retreat from everyday life is valuable, even necessary, especially when we experience overstimulation in our often highly scheduled and very busy life. We may find our relationships do not seem as fulfilling, our job is unsatisfying, or personal interests seem to fade. This could be a sign that we are experiencing a type of burnout that would benefit greatly from a temporary period of withdrawing for a time to experience quiet and stillness. This time of withdrawal and reflection is also an important aspect of the spiritual journey and heightens the opportunity for us to experience pure awareness.

For some, the path of silence and contemplation is their life's work and is in no way inferior to the path of full involvement in the world. They are not two paths, although they appear to be quite different on the surface. Having surrendered completely the fantasy of self-determination, we recognize that for the rest of our lives, we are an instrument of God's will. Divine guidance that is always present reveals our perfectly timed next step.

Radical Self-Acceptance

When we face traumatic events, we can maintain perspective and composure by total acceptance of all that is. What would such total acceptance be like? How would it feel? Total acceptance can be described by paraphrasing a famous Zen saying, *When hungry, I eat;*

when thirsty I drink. To say it in the current context, *When sad I am completely sad; when angry I am completely angry.*

We have such a hard time accepting who and what we are. We need to engage in radical self-acceptance which includes total recognition and appreciation of any thought, feeling, or bodily sensation in its fullness, exactly as it is. This self-acceptance also includes an understanding that we have legitimate and healthy needs as a human being that deserve to be met in order to fulfill our human nature.

Feelings are not right or wrong. Becoming completely aware of the full intensity of our feelings is invaluable, though expressing our feelings in their full intensity is rarely indicated or beneficial. It is important to understand exactly how upset we are in each situation before we can begin to change or moderate our reactions to it.

Once we completely accept our feelings just as they are, it becomes possible to reduce our reactivity by learning to perceive and interpret events in a more objective and neutral light. Over time and with practice, seemingly traumatic events may provoke no emotional upset whatsoever.

Chapter Nine

ARE THERE OBSTACLES TO AWAKENING?

Hawk soars river sighs
Follow me where night turns day
Inside out upside down

Does a soaring hawk experience obstacles? What if the hawk is hungry? Is hunger an obstacle or merely an indication to search for food? Can we be one with our life, eating when hungry, sleeping when tired? The awake mind is taut like a drawn bow. Watch the hawk. Does it daydream, creating wistful fantasies of imaginary pasts and futures?

To find, we must passionately seek until seeking lets go on its own. It is usually not a conscious or deliberate giving up initiated by our thinking mind. It is more of an involuntary surrender because the body-mind simply cannot push any further. In my early days of teaching this awareness, I would emphasize the aspect of unearned grace which seemed to appear on its own, freely given. I could discern no clear causal relationship between awakening and my own effort. While grace is very real and absolutely necessary, my overemphasis on this aspect led some people to believe they did not have to do anything at all, except maybe listen to me talk about it. Wrong! It is critical to strive with all your heart, or as Jesus says with complete clarity in Mark 12:30: *Love the Lord your God with all your heart and with all your soul and with all your mind and with all your strength.* It is up to us to do everything we can, understanding that the final step is more than we can accomplish on our own, and happens through the grace of God.

From the Absolute perspective, there are no fixed, unyielding obstacles to awakening. Nor is there anything to experience, or one to experience it. There is nothing to seek and nothing to find. No one was ever lost. Therefore, there are no obstacles. All perceived obstacles are nothing but thoughts in our minds, erroneous beliefs that may be deeply entrenched but are false. These thoughts, like most thoughts, have no value and are not true at the nondual level.

Speaking from a Relative or dualistic perspective, some thoughts and beliefs are obviously true, and even valuable, and some are false. For example, it's true in the relative sense that I typed this sentence on a desktop computer. It is also true that there are 12 inches in a foot. This measurement is factually accurate because we have agreed on it, not because it is an absolute truth in the universe. Knowledge and information are valuable and allow us to function in our culture. It is important to distinguish between the Absolute and the Relative perspective when discussing the highest spiritual truth. The best spiritual teaching flows freely between both, with the direct knowing that both are only partially true. We are all thoroughly familiar with the dualistic or relative way of thinking, perceiving, and interpreting our world. This is the province of traditional religions, Newtonian physics, and conventional ways of knowing. It certainly matters, but it is only part of what matters. Since we all are familiar with the relative perspective, it is often not accentuated in spiritual teaching about awakening.

When our eyes are open, each thing reveals itself continuously exactly as it is, with nothing added or subtracted. Things simply are as they are. Life does not need our input to fix it. We will never open our eyes by thinking about opening our eyes. Nothing in the universe needs to be any different, ever, including us. Therefore, from the Absolute perspective there is no need to awaken and no one to awaken. However, for reasons that are truly mysterious, some of us are compelled to seek for this imaginary experience of awakening. It is imaginary because we cannot possibly know what it is ahead of time. Yet, after we experience some degree of awakening, it is both life altering and almost impossible to explain.

Awakening is the end of the one who seeks, nothing more and nothing less. It is not an experience, and not a state. Your true nature is unchanging, and neither deepens nor becomes shallower but is continuous, unbroken, and always the same. Nothing is separate or outside it. Nothing is right or wrong, there is no up or down, you and me, and no before or after. Nothing becomes more aware or less aware. In fact, nothing becomes or ceases to be anything at all. It has no qualities that can be described.

To awaken is to lose permanently all interest in becoming something other than what we currently are. There are no questions to ask and no one to ask them. Nothing needs doing or undoing. Nothing needs improving. Seeking and the one who seeks finally end. Time, space, matter, substance, boundaries, phenomenal existence, birth, and death all end.

For this reason, all perceived obstacles are simply fear-based objections to the profound dissolution of all that we currently know. This complete and permanent dissolution is understandably threatening to the self-identity because its entire purpose is to continue its imaginary existence. The self-identity will never seek its own demise because it can only want a new and improved version of itself or its circumstances. This is the usual reason for beginning the spiritual search, namely, to develop an improved version of ourselves. Of course, there is nothing wrong with improving ourselves in meaningful ways. Self-improvement and awakening are simply two very different realities. Awakening is the end of *me,* as thinking mind defines me. Jed McKenna (2002, p. 265) has said that if you knew what it was, you wouldn't want it!

Many people have very reasonable questions and objections to this understanding. They believe that gradual, progressive self-improvement and purification is a worthy goal and will eventually lead to awakening. Nothing is wrong or right with self-improvement and purification practices. In fact, such work in some form is probably required as long as we are alive. If we have a body and a mind that are born and die, we will have an ego or self-identity. The ego dies only when this body and mind cease. Even after a profound and enduring awakening, deep-seated, automatic habits and beliefs continue and must be observed and deconstructed. After awakening this work becomes much easier, for then we no longer live in a fantasy world created by our thinking mind, although as human beings we may occasionally want to visit!

> *Q: What is sudden illumination?*
> *A: 'Sudden' means ridding ourselves of deluded thoughts instantaneously. 'Illumination' means the realization that illumination is not something to be attained.*
> Ch'an Master Hui Hai (Blofeld, J., 2007, p. 43).

Our self-identity finds reassurance in the belief that through various practices, reading, thinking, and visiting spiritual teachers, gradual progress towards genuine awakening occurs. Slow, gradual improvement is appealing because it allows the self to maintain the illusion that it controls life. The radical, sudden, all-at-once nature of real awakening is too threatening and incomprehensible for the self to grasp. A few of the most common beliefs and misconceptions about perceived obstacles to awakening are discussed below.

The Path Is Too Hard

On hearing it, many of his disciples said,
'This is a hard teaching. Who can accept it?

John 6:60

Awakening to who and what we are, always have been, and cannot not be is not easy. It is simple in a way, but hard to grasp, much less realize. However, to continue living in a created dream world takes much more effort and energy than living in reality as it is. Imagine living a life without problems, with nothing to worry or be concerned about. Thinking occurs only when necessary and is used to answer actual questions, not to create elaborate imaginary scenarios in the mind. There is nothing simpler than refraining from second-guessing past decisions of our own or others.

In the awakened state, we know directly and unequivocally for ourselves that all is perfect and is exactly the way it should be. Nothing is unkind or unfair and there is no sense of entitlement or corresponding frustration and disappointment that we did not get what we deserved. We rarely experience anger towards other people because we accept and realize that they are who they are instead of who we want them to be. We do not experience anger towards ourselves because we accept that we are who we are instead of who we believe we should be. These statements are made in an absolute manner, and no one is fully like this, but it gives you a sense of why this path is worth the effort.

I Do Not Have Time to Awaken

Nothing is right or wrong with living our life the way we choose. However, we do have some choice in pursuing this Great Matter of waking up to our true nature.

Our ordinary understanding of time is a conditioned belief. Like all our conditioned beliefs, our understanding of time limits and constricts our natural freedom of direct action. Yet, we always have enough time to stop creating fantasies in our head, because that effort does not take much time at all.

According to some ancient spiritual traditions, awakening is said to occur in the gap between the inhalation and the exhalation of one breath, for that is the time when the mind is naturally quietest. When we see through breathing in and breathing out, we see through birth and death, me and you, before and after, now and then, and we see that all time and no time are not two.

It can also help us persist in this admittedly somewhat arduous path to realize that our efforts benefit not only us and everyone with whom we interact, but all beings, going both backwards and forwards in time. This truth becomes more apparent and less weird once we realize the relative nature of constructs such as space and time.

Whenever one human being, assisted by grace, experiences the clarity of vision described here, all beings benefit. Each being that awakens to the direct awareness of God's continuous Presence in the world makes it a tiny bit easier for everyone else who has yet to consciously know this experience.

I Will Not Be Able to Carry Out My Responsibilities

Awakening is the experience of an internal shift in perception, not an external change in our ability to be responsible individuals. While the moment of awakening itself is always sudden, it can take time, perhaps years, to integrate this profound realization into the activities of daily living. The seamless integration that allows us to live effortlessly, fully trusting in our no-mind knowing, speaking and acting, is progressive. Relaxation into and trust of this new way of life cannot be hurried.

Priorities do change, as trivial and meaningless pursuits gradually fall away on their own. It is likely that some activities, friends, and interests will naturally fall away as we live more fully in the world of what is real and spend less time in a fantasy world of our thinking mind's creation. Our goal, then, is to be present for what is real. Life will then effectively guide us towards those people, places, and activities that are most fulfilling and in accord with our true nature.

All activities are sacred from the Absolute perspective, with nothing inherently better or worse than anything else. From the Relative perspective, however, some choices are always better than others. In awakening, we realize the Absolute and Relative are not two, but blend seamlessly as one.

My Mind Is Too Busy to Meditate or Pray

The problem is not that we cannot meditate. The problem is that when we pay attention to the content of our mind, we are alarmed by the noise and chaos, which we cannot silence. As we learn how to be still inside, we realize that thoughts will always come and go, but remaining in our center of silence maintains the sense of serenity that a chattering mind denies us. The practice of internal silence is a wonderful definition of what the experience of meditation is.

Meditation is often a difficult practice because we have forgotten how to be still, silent, unmoving. We need to practice deliberately remembering and working at being a human being. This is why meditation is called a practice. By the time we reach adulthood, most of us have completely forgotten how to recognize this internal silence as an inherent part of who we are. We literally forget who we are moment-to-moment by believing in the content of our minds, and the constructed sense of self that is the self-identity or thinking mind. By worshipping our own mind, we distance ourselves from experiencing more fully the kingdom of heaven. When we pay attention to our thinking mind instead of the directly revealed Mind of Christ or Buddha Mind, we perpetuate our own emotional suffering. This internal silence is truly our natural state, even though it does not seem to come naturally to any of us. The practice of meditation helps us eventually realize that this internal state of silence is always here, ready and waiting for us to embrace it. As stated in Psalm 23:5, the table is prepared for us. We do not earn it or deserve it, yet it is freely and continuously given.

Meditation, prayer, contemplation, fasting, silent retreats, and all the other staples of the spiritual life are not necessarily required to know this truth. For most of us, though, these profound spiritual practices performed with the utmost devotion will benefit us enormously as they help quiet the objections of the self-identity to this often difficult and challenging work. The ego or self-identity wants what it wants, when it wants it. Nothing impedes our journey towards the realization of our natural state of internal silence more than the ongoing activity of our self-absorbed mind. The more we dwell in silence, the more we will lose interest in our thinking mind. We then become aware that our entire life has become a continuous prayer. Only at that point do we fulfill the Apostle Paul's injunction to *Pray without ceasing*. Resting in internal silence allows us to dwell directly in the presence of God, making our life a living prayer.

I Do not Want to Live Life Like a Monk

Spiritual awakening has often been confused with many activities that have no connection to it. For example, we often mistake unfamiliar cultural and religious practices for signs of awakening. A shaved head, funny robes or strange names have nothing to do with authentic spiritual practice. Nor does the authentic path require deprivation of ordinary human pleasures. In fact, abstaining from ordinary pleasures serves no purpose other than to feed the self-absorbed ego. There is a particular form of spiritual pride that thrives on feeling superior because of the depth of self-deprivation endured. Question everything proposed to you as a necessary practice. Most activities unfamiliar to Western minds are not required. These activities should only be engaged in because we have a desire to do so and see some clear benefit, not because we believe it is a requirement for spiritual awakening.

The Pain of Identity Deconstruction

> *Its fire pit has been made deep and wide, with an abundance of fire and wood;*
> *the breath of the Lord, like a stream of burning sulfur, sets it ablaze.*
>
> Isaiah 30:33

> *Jesus said, I have thrown fire on the world. Look! I watch it until it blazes.*
>
> The Gospel of Thomas, 10

In her book *Perfect Madness: From Awakening to Enlightenment*, Donna Lee Gorrell (Inner Ocean, 2001) describes her painful and confusing self-deconstruction process, which mostly covered a period of about nine months in the early 1970s when she was only 23 years old. The book begins somewhat ominously: *I was naïve when my spiritual journey began. I wanted growth without change, wisdom without experience, security without sacrifice, and life without death. I wanted to swim in the waters of eternity without getting wet* (p. 1). Being born again in the real sense is a profoundly destabilizing experience. It rarely occurs without some degree of fallout.

Jesus said, I will destroy this house, and no one will be able to build it again.
The Gospel of Thomas, 71

Some people going through this radical deconstruction process of waking up to what is real have their entire life fall apart as things start to heat up. For an interesting and enlightening description of just how powerful and destabilizing this deconstruction process can be, see Margot Ridler's eBook *True Freedom versus Self-Improvement: A Life Without Suffering Can Be Yours* (2019).

As the deconstruction process takes hold, there may be profound psychological and physical symptoms. Various symptoms, infinite in their variety, can emerge and are best understood as a somewhat predictable part of the ego deconstruction process. Without the context of intense inner spiritual work, they are routinely seen from a conventional perspective and treated as such by mainstream physicians and psychotherapists.

I believe that the period from the first real glimpse of nondual awareness until the emergence of a stable, continuous dwelling in this awareness is what St. John of the Cross meant by the Dark Night of the Soul. The last 40 or so years of Mother Teresa's life can best be understood as one long and harrowing dark night as she felt bereft and abandoned by God (Kolodiejchuk, B. (Ed.), 2007). Her devotional commitment in the face of this prolonged spiritual drought is remarkable. The wandering pilgrim can be helped immeasurably by an accurate understanding of the various symptoms that can emerge. Mother Teresa benefitted from access to a spiritual confessor who understood the Dark Night aspects of her struggle.

Perhaps with this background we can revisit the idea of fire and brimstone in the Old Testament. Maybe these frightening images of devastation are not merely descriptions of the suffering awaiting sinners who veer from the path as many of us were taught. What if the real path inevitably involves flames, smoke and destruction? Periodic fires are necessary for a living forest to restore itself as deadwood and choking undergrowth are removed. Attachments to aspects of the former life often must be surrendered. The deeply entrenched self-identity does not usually give up without a fierce fight. Once a serious and committed spiritual search is commenced, we may experience times of feeling as if we are alone in the desert, or times that we might describe as a dark night of the soul. These times are when we are being restored as our own spiritual blindness is removed. Now the passage from Isaiah 30:33 *the breath of the Lord, like a stream of burning sulfur, sets it ablaze* can be seen from a new perspective.

Spiritual seeking, at least in a superficial sense, has become acceptable, even popular in some circles. There can now be an ego-based gratification in seeking because of the fallacies we believe to be true about the spiritual journey. Some of these fallacies include:

- Believing that being a spiritual seeker means that we are somehow special and are therefore relieved of ordinary expectations to function in society as productive and responsible adults.
- Viewing the spiritual journey itself as indisputable evidence of moral superiority to everyone else.
- Believing that to be a serious spiritual seeker we must live very marginal lives, barely eking out a subsistence existence and appearing to avoid responsibilities in the real world as much as possible.

In fact, functioning in society as productive and responsible adults, believing that no one is superior to anyone else, and accepting any and all our responsibilities in the real world are all valid and worthy methods of practicing the Way.

There is a mystique conveyed by teachers and traditions profoundly different from ours. Western spiritual seekers may falsely assume that only Asian or Indian teachers of Buddhism or Hinduism have the spiritual goods. Frequently, nothing could be further from the truth. Americans and Westerners in general are naïve and frequently unskilled at determining genuine spiritual wisdom. The development of discernment is facilitated as we learn to treasure stillness and become more in tune with our own inner knowing.

I have now been an observer and participant in the spiritual marketplace for nearly 50 years, and have seen an explosion of interest, much of it very sincere. As in every activity, it is important to use intuition, careful observation, skepticism and discernment to evaluate teachers and practices. With clever marketing pigs can indeed appear to fly! I have found one clear marker to assist in determining which teachers to take to heart. When listening to a teacher, does your mind naturally tend to become still and quiet? If so, you are probably in the presence of an awakened being who can effectively communicate this understanding. There are other markers but look for this one first. It the teacher does not routinely transmit their intuitive understanding by their energetic presence, it is usually best to look elsewhere.

Genuine awakening is no respecter of religion, race, culture, language, tradition, lineage, gender, age, or anything else the dualistic mind can dream up. We owe a deep debt of gratitude to the Eastern traditions for developing and sustaining the spiritual knowledge that facilitates the development of genuine insight into our true nature. In awakening, we understand the old Zen adage that states, *my nose is vertical, my eyebrows horizontal.* Nothing special in one way, yet what could be more radical and revolutionary?

It is important to not neglect our own religious traditions and practices. When seen with fresh eyes, we already have everything we need in our own traditional religious practices. It is also true that our Christian and Jewish approaches to religious practice have benefited enormously from cross fertilization with ancient Eastern meditative traditions. An example is the Contemplative Prayer work developed by Father Thomas Keating and his Benedictine brothers.

The Importance of Commitment

It's important to make a serious and passionate commitment to awaken in this lifetime for the benefit of all beings. This commitment will invoke all manner of support, seen and unseen, to assist us on our journey. However, depriving ourselves of ordinary human pleasures is not the way. Shakyamuni Buddha tried the ascetic approach of severe self-deprivation and nearly died in the process. The Buddha described his path as the Middle Way between self-indulgence and self-deprivation. It was while practicing in this manner that he had his great awakening.

We may erroneously glorify self-deprivation as a spiritual practice. We can easily inflate our self-identity when we purposely deprive ourselves. This is the same kind of gratification found in the deprivation addictions, such as food anorexia, sexual anorexia, and workaholism. The internal high from these deprivation addictions comes from the fallacy that the self-discipline required to deny ourselves what others seem to need proves to our ego that it is superior to all other egos.

Self-deprivation of ordinary human pleasures is often a way to aggrandize and inflate our self-identity. This is one major reason that the true path is so difficult for the ordinary ego or thinking mind to grasp. The ego is always looking for ways to become more than and superior to other egos. The true nature of the spiritual path is to move further and further away from this falsehood. As we progress, we are both more aware of our faults and more compassionate about our limitations as denial gradually recedes.

We may need to withdraw for a time from our usual activities, take a break from our daily routine and be in solitude. Temporarily, this is fine if we are led to do so. This period of self-imposed solitude may facilitate the erosion of interest in the meaningless activities of the mind. We must always find our own way and follow our own instincts as to what is in our best interest and, accordingly, for the best and highest good of all.

Spiritual geniuses such as Jesus Christ, Shakyamuni Buddha, Abraham, Moses, Muhammad and others have done their best to teach and describe the direct path. Unfortunately, their teachings are often distorted and misunderstood by those who create and believe in spiritual rules, rituals, regulations, laws, injunctions, requirements, and prohibitions. These distortions of the original, directly revealed truth are not the true Way.

Chapter Ten

Is Suffering Beneficial?

Out of suffering may come a transmutation of values, even the transfiguration of character. But these developments are possible only if the man cooperates. If he does not, then the suffering is in vain, fruitless.
Paul Brunton (1984, p. 157).

To have any hope of awakening to our true nature in this life, we must arouse intense energy and maintain a relentless focus on an impossible-to-understand goal. We must strive relentlessly without knowing how to do so. An acute awareness of our own and others' suffering is necessary for most of us to begin this process. A continuing awareness of suffering is essential for this passionate commitment to persist. Nothing else will be sufficiently motivating.

Therefore, give thanks for the suffering you experience. Suffering is truly our best friend in the spiritual search. As we make progress on the spiritual path, we will become progressively calmer and more peaceful, and our suffering will diminish.

For those who experience life as comfortable and content, and who nevertheless wish to journey down the spiritual path, it can be helpful to carefully consider the immense suffering of other humans, animals, trees, rivers, and Mother Earth as a whole.

It is certainly possible to mitigate the personal experience of suffering by following spiritual practices even if we do not experience awakening as part of our journey. An important challenge on this journey, however, is to push beyond our personal comfort level. It will be tempting to discontinue the journey if we feel a significant amount of discomfort. While reducing effort and commitment in the face of difficulty might enhance our comfort, it will also deny us further growth and the possible experience of awakening.

We need to have faith that it is possible for us to awaken to the truth of our being. This faith is the recognition and belief that others have traversed this path with varying degrees of success and that we can do the same. Carrying that faith, we can move into areas of spiritual exploration that may challenge us or make us feel anxious and uncomfortable.

Repeated exposure to true teachings is helpful. In Buddhism, these teachings are the Dharma, initially presented by the historic Buddha, Shakyamuni. Many of these classic Buddhist teachings were present centuries earlier in Hindu and Chinese scriptures and is readily available today in the classic texts of spiritual wisdom such as the *Bhagavad Gita*, the *Ashtavakra Gita,* and the *Tao Te Ching*.

Some people find their spiritual journey is enhanced by having deep religious faith and a devotional practice. Others take this journey without being connected to a particular faith expression. Each of us must find what works best on our own path. Regardless of the tools we use on the journey, it is important to have an acute awareness of and sensitivity towards the experience of suffering.

The Reality of Suffering

It is extremely difficult for us to think clearly about suffering because we are determined to be separate from it. We become anxious if we think about suffering because of our deep-seated fear it could happen to us. We fear being out of control of how much suffering we will endure, what type of suffering will occur, and how intense the suffering will be. Therefore, when it happens to others, we can engage in minimizing or even denying suffering's existence. We can say with great relief, *there but for the grace of God go I*. It is tempting to pretend that real suffering is something that happens to other people. When suffering arises in our loved ones or in us, it may be minimized and denied, or grossly exaggerated. There is rarely a sensitive appreciation and acceptance of the reality of suffering, much less of the potential benefits of enduring suffering with the grace of awareness. Our natural denial and avoidance of the subject does not help us confront suffering directly and honestly. For us to be fully present to all that is real in the world, we must include suffering for us to be fully human.

The problem of suffering has challenged and perplexed theologians and other religious thinkers. For an interesting perspective on the difficulty traditional religions experience with the issue of suffering see Bart Ehrman's book *God's Problem: How the Bible Fails to Answer Our Most Important Question-Why We Suffer* (2008). In this book Ehrman provides an excellent critical analysis of the general failure of traditional religions to provide meaningful answers to the issue of suffering.

The Root of Suffering

Simply put, the real root of our suffering is our very human, very real false sense of entitlement. We take our entitlement for granted and rarely question it. The typical assumption underlying this entitlement is that we deserve reality to be the way we want it to be. The primary cause of much of our frustration in life comes from taking our beliefs and opinions seriously and believing they are true. What follows are a myriad of physical and emotional reactions to the belief that our closely held assumptions and convictions are in accord with reality.

SUGGESTED PRACTICE

Take a few minutes now to reflect on your personal entitlement delusions. Over the past week, how has your sense of entitlement created hardship for you? Remember specific instances when you felt offended, mistreated, or disrespected. Remember the times you felt hurt. Consider ways you could have felt about the experience other than hurt or offended.

Replay in your mind an interaction that made you feel hurt or offended. Become aware of your desire to justify your reaction. Then ask yourself these questions:

1. *Are you aware of an argumentative tone in your head?*
2. *Do you want to be right?*
3. *Do you want the other to be wrong?*
4. *Does making these judgments improve your sense of well-being?*
5. *Do you have to make such judgments or is it merely a bad habit?*
6. *How many times have you previously replayed this scene in your mind?*
7. *Did replaying it ever, even once, lead to an improvement in your mood?*
8. *Imagine for a moment that you somehow lost interest in forming these self-aggrandizing rationalizations for your feelings. What would that be like? Would your life be more enjoyable?*

Our false sense of entitlement holds these beliefs: we should never be disappointed, live with uncertainty, or even be uncomfortable. We firmly believe that reality should be the way we want it to be, and for that reason we suffer. When we fight reality, we lose every time. Effective and skillful action can come only from our direct seeing of what is true. Clear seeing is possible only after we have let go of our self-centered, entitled views. Seeing clearly what is real we find peace and become a force for good in the world. When we see this truth and begin to manifest it in our conduct in the world, we literally become bringers of light, giving meaning to our life and fulfilling our destiny. All beings benefit from the slightest effort made to realize our true nature.

Serving Others

In awareness, we do not deny suffering, and we do not feel oppressed or burdened by the very real suffering we see around us and in the news. We wish to serve, in some manner, those who suffer through our naturally arising feelings of compassion. Serving others comes naturally to us and can be mutually beneficial if the wish to serve arises freely from awareness. In this case there are not two parties-one who is serving and one who is being served. There is merely the free movement of awareness in the world, doing what is needed in the most skillful manner possible. The one appearing to provide service would not feel superior to the one receiving service.

Some mistakenly believe they should not enjoy life when so many are hungry and homeless. Depriving ourselves of happiness and contentment does not make anyone's life better. It does not make us more spiritual because we take on and experience the suffering of others. If our eyes are open, we will always see suffering around us. While it is important to see suffering as it is, nothing is gained, and no one is helped if we deny that suffering exists or if we attempt to carry the burden of it for others.

It is important to note that some attempts to help others may do little other than to make their situation worse. Any number of reasons may account for this including our mistaken assumptions about what someone else needs and wants. In fact, we rarely know what is best for ourselves, much less for another person. When we think we know what someone needs and try to help them from that perspective, resentment can easily be the result on both sides. The helper feels a sense of obligation and is puzzled by the seeming lack of gratitude from the recipients. The recipient may feel overwhelmed by dire need and resentful that aid is not more predictable and skillfully targeted to their real needs. This does not mean that service to those in need is wrong. It means the assistance needs to be done mindfully and with sensitivity to the ever-changing needs of the recipients.

We need to notice the multitude of thoughts, feelings, and reactions that occur within ourselves when we endeavor to provide help. Conversely, we also need to notice, with as much objectivity as possible, the full range of reactions from the person we are attempting to help. If we feel compelled to help someone, then we should do what we think is right, but our efforts will be most successful if we do not assume that we know what is best for others. By losing interest in our own self-absorbed and repetitive thoughts, we will become far more aware of what others may truly need and not what we think or assume they need. Only then will it be possible to provide genuinely helpful assistance to others.

It is not possible to provide specific, concrete guidelines for behavior in every situation, because each situation is unique. If our efforts to give are truly free, we will have no sense of having given. Consequently, there is no sense of pride or self-inflation for having helped someone. The experience of giving is free, automatic, and largely effortless. Everyone's life has value and meaning, regardless of how that life may seem to us. An individual may be doing exactly what is needed to progress spiritually in the fastest way currently available. We have no need to judge another person's life situation. Continuous humility, a willingness to be open and to learn, and deep respect for the unique challenges faced by others will serve us well.

Healing ourselves first is always good advice. Notice how quickly we rush to judgment about another's life. Accept that what is valuable to them may be radically different from what is valuable to us. We almost never know for sure what is best for another person.

Recognition of this fact does not mean that we withhold help and support where we observe it might be needed and wanted. Helping when we can, in a way where our help is welcomed and needed is a good thing. However, worrying about another's misfortune is often, believe it or not, nothing but self-centered indulgence. This understanding is the complete opposite from what we usually assume to be true. Action directed toward the alleviation of suffering may be beneficial but misery over the imagined or real suffering of others is without merit. Worry does not alleviate suffering. Instead, worry about others wellbeing needlessly creates suffering in the worrier who is trying to help. When we are lost in worry and rumination, we are not present for the reality of our life and cannot see another person accurately. Without the clear seeing that emerges from real presence, we are prone to provide help that is not needed or wanted. When we are carefully attuned to the reality of the situation, the help we provide will be welcomed and appreciated.

Pain and Suffering

St. Teresa of Avila noted that pain is never permanent. Shakyamuni Buddha said that the unenlightened life is painful, and many other well-known spiritual teachers have said the same thing in various ways. The Buddha did not say that life is nothing but suffering and misery, for to be certain, everyone's life has wonderful moments. However, if we really look at our lives, we learn that we struggle endlessly, first to gain and then to hold onto those people, experiences, and material comforts that seem necessary for our contentment and satisfaction. We simultaneously strive endlessly to avoid those experiences we do not want. It is ceaseless and for most people this endless struggle of craving and aversion only ends with death.

Everything that we struggle so ceaselessly to gain, we will eventually lose. This realization seems depressing to most people and yet is obviously true. How do we come to terms with this truth? We define ourselves by the endless process of becoming and attaining. It begs the question: If we did not try so hard to attain what we want; how would we live our life? Who would we be? What if we simply allowed life to provide us what is needed and to remove what is no longer of benefit?

The freedom that comes with awakening to what is real liberates us from this endless striving. It is a joy to listen to people from the perspective of needing nothing and having nothing to prove or accomplish. It is also a rare experience to receive such attuned and compassionate attention from another. Most of us never listen in a state of pure presence to anyone. Similarly, we rarely experience someone listening to us with pure presence awareness. Normally, we as the listener or the person listening to us will have some personal goal or agenda to achieve. Awakening is the end of striving and the cessation of questioning. It allows us to have a better opportunity to listen without a strong feeling of separation.

In direct awareness, we will intuitively know everything we need to know. Knowing more facts, information, ideas, and beliefs are the stuff of our day-to-day life, but in direct awareness this kind of knowing will hold little interest for us unless it is needed. Seeing clearly, we no longer wonder about the meaning or purpose of life. Thus, over time, much of our psychological, existential, or psychic pain gradually disappears as deeply conditioned beliefs are progressively deconstructed.

Physical Pain

Pain and suffering are different. For the purposes of this discussion, let us define pain as unwanted physical sensations in our body. Pain is neither good nor bad; it just is. Suffering is the interpretation we put on the sensations of pain. If we resist and resent being in physical pain, if we judge it as being unfair or unbearable, we will add some measure of suffering to the physical reality of pain. Our thinking mind creates the suffering aspect of pain, based on our beliefs and expectations. If we have a belief that we should not have pain, then when we do have pain, we inevitably add a large measure of suffering to it. The pain itself may be inescapable, but suffering is optional.

This perspective may seem cold, callous, and lacking in compassion, but it is the best approach to living with inescapable pain. Our goal is to see things as they are. Many problems lose their power once they are seen clearly, accurately and objectively. It is only when we see clearly that we can be truly compassionate. In our efforts to be of service to those who are suffering, it is not helpful to be overwhelmed ourselves. The lack of self-acceptance, especially where unacceptable feelings are concerned, creates needless problems and produces no benefits.

An excellent description of how denial, emotional numbing, and dissociation affect our body is found in the brilliant work of John Sarno, MD (1998). Dr. Sarno's books deserve close study by anyone coping with chronic pain and as well as those who attempt to help them. His understanding of pain is the result of careful observation of patients he treated for many decades as a physician specializing in rehabilitation medicine.

In the course of his long medical practice Dr. Sarno came to realize that most chronic pain is the direct result of muscular bracing. This muscle tension, in turn, leads to a reduction in blood flow and oxygen to the affected muscle, resulting in very real pain. This pain, however, is the result of oxygen deprivation resulting from muscular bracing and inflammation. This muscular constriction is often the result of an inability or unwillingness to accept powerful emotions, such as resentment, anger, or grief. The lack of conscious acceptance of powerful feelings is a result of an internal, unconscious judgment that it is wrong to have such feelings, especially in such an intense way. It can be especially hard to recognize, much less accept feelings of anger and resentment when the target of the feelings is a loved one, such as an elderly parent.

The unconscious and erroneous belief we share is that a good and kind person would not have feelings of resentment, rage, or bitterness, certainly not towards a loved one. Yet being human, we all do have a range of potentially messy, unappealing feelings and reactions. We routinely lack simple self-compassion and self-forgiveness, yet we expect others to shower us with love and acceptance. We need to learn to be at peace and more accepting of ourselves exactly as we are. Being simply and thoroughly human takes us a long way down the spiritual path. When we insist on pretending to be more or better than we are, we create needless suffering for ourselves and others.

The Reality of Death

Death happens to everyone, but we like pretending it will not happen to us, at least not for a very long time, if ever! The truth is that we do not know how much longer we will be alive. Death can happen to anyone at any time. This is a difficult truth to face yet living with this reality can provide a needed motivation for spiritual practice. Early in my Zen training I remember hearing that the purpose of this hard practice is to prepare ourselves to die. While that notion did not sound appealing at the time, I gradually came to appreciate the inherent wisdom of this statement. So much seemingly needless suffering occurs at the end of life as the dying person and their loving family and friends struggle to cope with the inevitability of death. It is highly recommended to face the reality of death when we are healthy and have the biological and psychic energy for this difficult work.

Among many other benefits, spiritual growth helps develop an acceptance of things as they are, including the fact that we will ultimately die. Nothing is wrong with death. Death is only a problem if we wish to continue in the state of being physically alive! When we see things as they are and accept all that is, death is just another experience, neither good nor bad. The fear of death is at the very core of many self-destructive behaviors. Only in facing the truth of our own mortality can we truly live. We need to fully live until we fully die.

Why not Die Now?

Jesus Christ and Shakyamuni Buddha, as well as others, have taught how to end suffering. The magic prescription is to die now in the spiritual sense, die completely and radically to all our conditioned, programmed beliefs about who and what we are. This spiritual death allows entry to the Garden of Eden, which has always been right before our eyes. It is here, now, not someplace else in a different time or place. This spiritual death is not a biological or physical death. It is far more radical. The death and rebirth in the spirit Jesus refers to is the death of the false but deeply conditioned, unconscious, automatic concept of who we are. Everyone dies physically. It happens when causes and conditions are right. The spiritual death and rebirth referred to here is vastly more difficult but can occur in this lifetime. Jesus Christ tells us,

The Kingdom of God doesn't come with our careful observation, nor will people say, 'Here it is,' or 'There it is,' because the kingdom of God is within you.

Luke 17:20

There is nowhere else the kingdom of God could be except within ourselves.

Diminishing Suffering

By applying the commonsense principles discussed within the pages of this book, our own suffering will diminish as will the harm we are capable of inflicting on others. The benefits of applying these principles will become real for anyone who takes these observations seriously. Contributing directly to the welfare of all beings doesn't require awakening. It merely requires that we begin to pay attention and live outwardly in reality instead of inwardly in our mind where our self-identity rules. However, we exponentially magnify our ability to have a beneficial effect on the world as we see clearly our True Nature. Only with some level of self-realization can we understand that allowing our ego to control our behavior does nothing beneficial. It is only by reducing the power of the ego's grip on our thoughts, behaviors and perceptions that we can be an instrument of the will of God in the world. In doing so, we free ourselves from needless suffering and do not contribute to the suffering of others.

Chapter Eleven

HUMAN BEINGS ARE WANTING MACHINES

Happiness means getting what you want.

Really?

> *SUGGESTED PRACTICE*
>
> *Begin by sitting quietly with the focus of attention on your breath. Once your body-mind begins to settle a bit, reflect on times in your life where you got something or someone that you really wanted. What happened after your dream came true? We rarely question the validity of the deeply held assumption that getting our wishes fulfilled is beneficial. This is a belief that we have been programmed to trust, and it can govern and control our entire life.*
>
> *Now take a few minutes and reflect on times when you have struggled mightily to achieve a goal that seemed overwhelmingly important. Remember the fear and anxiety, as well as the exhilaration when you succeeded. Assume for a moment that struggling to achieve various goals in your life has been worthwhile. When does this struggle end? Why not now?*

If It Feels Good, Do It?

Coming of age in the 1960s, I heard cultural icons who seriously proposed doing exactly what you feel like doing with no thought to how such actions may affect anyone else. Since that time, it has become common to believe that we are entitled to do what we want, when we want. Today we rarely question the validity of the pursuit of narcissistic self-indulgence. We tend to worship the idea of self-fulfillment, but do we ever wonder about the nature of this self that so desperately wants to be fulfilled?

If we are acting in accord with the universal wisdom of Mind, our behavior comes not from our own conditioned self-gratification, but from no-mind or the true Self. The inner experience of this selfless action is an effortless, enjoyable, and effective engagement with the ordinary world. Our engagement with the world is naturally respectful of all life, not merely our own whims and ever-changing desires. When understood and interpreted in accord with universal wisdom, doing what truly feels good both emotionally and physically is being one with the will of God. When we listen to and act from our thinking mind or self-identity, the price we and others pay for the temporary gratification we receive is often painfully high.

When faced with a decision about what to do, why not ask: What is the will of God now, in this situation? It can also be very helpful to ask out loud: *Lord, please show me your will for me.* Doesn't it make sense to always strive to do the will of God instead of following our constantly changing self-indulgences?

Some American medical schools require their students to subscribe to the Declaration of Geneva, a revision and update of the traditional Hippocratic Oath. The encouragement to young doctors is to always hold in mind the best and highest result for the patient. Similarly, the term *ahimsa* in Hindu and Buddhist teachings means non-violence and respect for all sentient beings. No one is an island unto themselves. We are all profoundly interdependent. By acting with regard for the highest good for all we are simultaneously doing what is best for us as individuals. Self-centeredness is the problem, not the cure.

The Ultimate Cure

Most books on spirituality or psychological self-help focus on developing a new and improved version of the self-identity. It is good to effectively advocate for our legitimate needs. Much of my work as a psychotherapist involved helping people have reasonable personal boundaries and stand up for themselves. This work is important and beneficial. However, in the context of universal wisdom our goal is more expansive. We seek to transform the fundamental experience of the mind itself. This is a great challenge, yet it is not outside the realm of possibility.

Traditional religions usually teach that God is separate and fundamentally different from us. To assert our inherent oneness with the Creator of all that is would be heretical in some religions. In spiritual awakening, we see that the belief in a fundamental distinction between God and humans is false. God is always here, always now. For a variety of reasons, primarily ignorance of our true nature and misguided selfishness, we often do not notice God's continuous presence in our lives. To correct this mistake, all we must do is look and see what is real. God is never hidden. However, we must open our intuitive vision to see Him. The development of presence awareness is the healing balm that soothes problems and stresses of daily life. This presence awareness is the recognition of the continuous and all-pervading presence of the Divine and our oneness with the Creator.

What Is Presence?

The world's great religions call this presence *divine*. To understand it, we do not need to assume any kind of power separate from or outside of ourselves. This presence is our true nature. It is what we are, always have been, and cannot not be. We are born with *it*, as *it* is our human nature. We can never lose *it*, any more than we can lose our hands. *It* is as close to us as our breath. *It* never leaves us, although we can keep our wisdom eye tightly shut and pretend *it* is not here.

We all have had experiences of being fully present, absorbed and engaged in our lives. Such experiences are wonderful and inherently fulfilling. We fondly remember and treasure these special moments. A characteristic of presence awareness is complete absorption in this moment, as it is, usually with a lack self-awareness. Time seems to fly by without any experience of time passing. While we are totally absorbed, there is no self-consciousness, and this disappearance of self-consciousness is one of the main reasons why such experiences are so enjoyable. The inner chatter that is characteristic of our thinking mind stops on its own with no effort on our part. As the experience of presence awareness continues, there is an overall feeling of effortlessness. Nothing is especially difficult, and there is no sense of worry, tension, or fear.

This state is called *flow* and it is deeply rewarding. Anything we do that appears to elicit this state becomes compelling, almost addictive. It is the same experience as the runners high that runners sometimes experience. I experienced this effortless running as a sense of floating without effort during the last 5 minutes or so of my first 5-kilometer race. I will never forget the sheer delight of being completely alive and present, running freely, undisturbed. The running happened on its own with no sense that I was doing it.

Walking Freely, Undisturbed

We can also have this experience of presence awareness when we are doing absolutely nothing. It often seems to emerge when we are alone, although it can happen anywhere while doing anything. This spontaneous sense of flow may emerge more frequently when we are alone in a natural setting. It is very common to have this experience in childhood. I remember riding my bike for what seemed like endless hours with no awareness of time. Just riding, pumping my legs for sheer joy, going nowhere and anywhere. Hours would drift by. I was alone, but not lonely. The experience was one of joy and total contentment. In those days, parents felt no need to micromanage their children. I could roam free, without worry or concern.

Following the deep shift in consciousness that I experienced in 2002, I returned to the Rochester Zen Center for more meditation retreats. Driving home after the first retreat I attended after my return to intensive training, I had a vision of perfect beauty and oneness. I saw the star child that appeared at the end of the wonderful movie *2001: A Space Odyssey*. I received the insight that this blessed infant, gazing with wide-open eyes, was my own original Mind, open and free. This spontaneous, nonverbal insight into who and what *I AM* applies to every one of us. Our pure awareness is totally innocent, trusting, vulnerable, and naked in every way possible. Without defenses or boundaries, it has no need to justify or explain itself. I felt love for everyone during this vision as I recognized my own self as the Self of everyone and everything.

Absorption

We all have had experiences of timeless absorption in what is. It is very beneficial to pause to remember these moments of presence awareness. We must personally engage and experience these truths as opposed to just reading or hearing about them for real change within ourselves to occur. It's necessary to involve our entire being, including our body, mind, and feelings.

> *SUGGESTED PRACTICE*
>
> *Remember vividly a time in your life when you were internally quiet and absorbed completely in what you were doing. Bring this memory fully into conscious awareness now. Savor this memory, taste it, smell it, know and experience it fully. This is not only remembering but also experiencing. Feel in your body the awareness of freedom, joy, and timeless presence in the world. As you allow this vivid remembering to unfold, other similar memories may spontaneously arise. If this occurs, allow for and accept them. Notice how much more enjoyable these experiences are than our ordinary default setting of self-absorbed worry. Know through your own experiential awareness that you have the God-given right to live your life fully in a way that's satisfying and meaningful for you. Your life will then be in accord with the will of God.*

Artificial Insufficiency

Pop culture, which saturates our every waking moment, endlessly reminds us of the importance of getting what we want. The clear implication is that our life could be much more fulfilling if only we would change ourselves in some fundamental manner, often by buying some product or service. The idea that we are already whole and complete as we are does not sell many products. The function of advertising is to create the sense of lack or insufficiency where none previously existed. For an interesting discussion of how the marketing industry sells makeup by creating an artificial sense of lack in women, see *The Beauty Myth: How Images of Beauty Are Used Against Women* by Naomi Wolf (2002).

After Awakening

Everything continues as before after awakening. The difference is that virtually nothing is a problem. Things just are what they are. There's no longer a need for people, places, or things to be different from what they are. Mercifully, this realization applies to us also! The awareness is that all is well. Nothing needs to change. A phrase that popped into my head was *no one, going nowhere, doing nothing*. Life happens of its own, in its own way, at its own time. Obviously, there is no need to worry about anything when this is your experience. Life takes care of its own, and that includes you and me. We are guided, sheltered and protected in ways that we cannot imagine possible.

This internal perceptual shift is both radical and subtle. Although nothing has changed, everything is different. Searching deep inside, we cannot find the one we had always assumed we were. This awareness is the end of seeking and becoming. The lifelong project of being who we think we are supposed to be ceases. Everything happens, seemingly of its own, at the right time and in the best possible manner. Nothing can or should be any different than it is. People and things simply are what they are. There are no problems until our thinking mind steps in and starts comparing what is with what it believes should be but is not. This comparing process is the real root of suffering. Resisting the urge to compare what is with what is not eliminates our self-inflicted suffering. Our life does not need to be any different from what it already is. Just rest in *this* and be free. How delightful!

Chapter Twelve

ADDICTIONS ARE US

A person rarely sees his desires. They become apparent when his desires have a fight among themselves. The desire to get drunk will be countered by the desire to be free from drunkenness, or to be free from the consequences.

Rose, R. (2001), p. 76.

Every one of us is addicted to our conditioned mind and self-identity. In this way every one of us is an addict. Furthermore, for those of us who find ourselves thinking this is not true for them, it is important to remember that denial is the hallmark of addiction.

We can become emotionally or chemically addicted to people, experiences, substances, beliefs, and much more. Broadening the usual understanding of addiction does not diminish or minimize the power of substance addiction, such as alcohol or opiates. Anyone can benefit enormously from the spiritual insights of the 12-step programs like Alcoholics Anonymous. It can be far too easy for those of us who have no history of substance addiction to see ourselves as fundamentally different and superior to those who have and who do. The addiction model proposed in AA is incredibly helpful to people trying to manage out of control behavior that relates to substance abuse. Many of the important insights of AA also can be helpful to those of us without substance addictions.

The Seduction of Numbing

There are many ways we can numb ourselves, but dependence on addictive substances is among the most destructive. We numb ourselves to avoid the experience of ordinary emotions such as love, fear, and anger. Our pervasive self-numbing prevents us from knowing and experiencing our biological, physical, and emotional reality. Much of the difficulty we encounter during daily life is the direct result of this behavior which is a rejection of what is true for us. We believe that we should feel and need only what we believe we are supposed to feel and need. Can we learn to value all our experience, even the parts that are painful, embarrassing, shameful, or humiliating? Accepting and valuing what is, all of it, applies here and everywhere.

In a traditional Zen story, a Zen master and his senior student are watching the funeral procession of a deceased Zen master. Monks and laypeople reverently carry the master's coffin through the medieval streets of the ancient Japanese city. Observing this scene of pious devotion, the living master exclaims, *Look at all of those dead people carrying one live one!*

What a powerful statement to try to understand! In the New Testament, Jesus frequently teaches that it is necessary to die and be reborn *in the spirit* to achieve real life. The death and rebirth we seek in the experience of direct awakening results in our being spiritually, energetically and emotionally alive while we are biologically alive.

The Experience of Craving in Relationships

The feeling of craving is analogous to the feeling of being in love at the beginning of a new relationship. We project this feeling on to the loved one, and in doing so we feel whole and complete only when we are with the beloved. All romantic fantasies play upon this craving for the beloved. Romantic or sexual craving is fueled by the fallacy that something outside us can complete us. A related notion is the belief that we cannot tolerate not having the object of our desire. Both beliefs are false, but rarely examined.

The exhilarating romantic high sometimes present at the beginning of a relationship eventually fades, no matter how deeply in love we think we are. The high is based on a rush of specific neurotransmitters, including serotonin and dopamine, to take all the romance and fantasy out of it. When the swirling dust of this dizzying high fades, we begin to see clearly who our beloved truly is and discover that he or she may be very different from the fantasy we imagined them to be in the early days of the relationship. In a healthy relationship, this passionate love evolves slowly into companionate love. In this far less intensely erotic and far more stable form of love, we value the other for who he or she is. As such, this affectionate bond of companionate love can deepen indefinitely.

Most relationship difficulties are the direct result of wanting our partner to be someone other than who they really are. This cycle of unrealistic expectations of the partner coupled with the sense of entitlement results in intense disappointment when the partner does not live up to our impossible expectations. The resulting conflict is exacerbated by the belief that the partner should change in some way to meet these unrealistic expectations. Naturally, the other person inevitably resists all efforts to fix or improve them.

Similar issues occur in relationships that are not romantic as well, including parent-child, sibling, coworker, boss, clergy, friend, client, therapist or teacher. As we progress in our ability to see clearly who we are, the difficulties in our relationships tend to diminish. The more quickly we let go of unrealistic expectations of anyone else to be anyone other than who they really are, the more quickly we will find peace in the relationship and within ourselves.

Endless Craving

There is no high greater or more intense than the first high experienced from the use of an addictive substance. Every use that follows is an attempt to experience the intensity of that first high again. In the language of addiction, it is called chasing the high. The effort is futile, but in the search to recreate the original high an active addiction is born. The craving for that original high continues indefinitely and is something every addict fights every single day until they are truly born again via a radical spiritual transformation. Recovering addicts rely on the truth that using an addictive substance is a temporary, substance-induced altered state of consciousness. They also respect the fact that in moments of vulnerability their mind will try to convince them otherwise. To give in to the craving is to engage in a fruitless, obsessive search for a re-creation of the original ecstatic experience.

This craving for a return to the ecstatic state is why some authors refer to addiction as a kind of bizarre and distorted spiritual search. This model may help us also understand behavioral addictions. For example, listening carefully to compulsive gamblers reveals a craving for the high they have previously experienced. Non-addicts share in this experience when they routinely sacrifice the present and future to satisfy a desire to re-create an imagined past experience. This attempt will always fail. What is needed is the ability to let go of any control issues and to relax deeply, resting in awareness. In that way an opportunity to cultivate states of presence awareness arises. Resting in the presence of God is the natural antidote to craving.

In presence awareness, there is no anxiety, no striving to improve or to perform, and no success or failure. Just *this*, as it is, nothing more. In this natural and effortless awareness, the relentless internal critic becomes quiet. Imagine for a moment that the only way you know to quiet the ceaseless noise in your mind is to take an addictive substance. What would you do? One helpful way of understanding addictive, compulsive behavior is to see it as a search for internal peace. Helping addicts learn to calm and soothe themselves is a very important part of treatment and recovery. I am convinced this is the underlying reason we currently see so much addictive behavior. In allowing ourselves to sink into a deep rest, doing nothing, going nowhere, no energy is expended in self-judgment or judgment of others. There is no sense of lack, there is nothing to become, and there is nothing to improve. There is recognition that everything is as it should be. The experience is not an ecstatic high, but rather an experience of peaceful and quiet contentment. It is a feeling of *being home*.

Abstinence

Choosing to abstain from addictive, compulsive behaviors is a necessary first step in becoming a mature adult. It is also an important step on the path of spiritual awakening. Abstaining from compulsive, destructive behavior is not the same as depriving ourselves of ordinary life pleasures, although it may at first seem to be.

Normal human pleasures are not a problem in addiction recovery. However, abstinence from such pleasures can be. Addicts are unskilled in meeting their ordinary needs for friendship, companionship, affection, rest, relaxation, and self-nurturance. If not engaged in healthy outlets for satisfying such ordinary human needs, the recovering addict can easily become stuck in or addicted to deprivation. If this occurs, a *dry drunk* often emerges.

Dry drunk is Alcoholics Anonymous lingo used to describe the intensely lonely, bitter, and painful experience of someone who is sober, but only physically sober, and not yet healed at the deepest levels. AA and similar 12-step self-help groups describe the recovery model as a program of spiritual healing. The goal is not only a comfortable abstinence from addictive behavior, but also a spiritual rebirth. This rebirth is elusive but essential. Without it, the sober addict is to some degree a dry drunk, always one step away from relapse.

This rebirth occurs through grace. Grace emerges when the addict completely and involuntarily surrenders everything to God. A deep self-examination leads to the revelation that the addict is not now and never has been in charge of their life. This genuine realization results in a massive reduction in the narcissism that previously ruled their lives and informed their active addiction.

If we observe a dry drunk or an active addict, we will notice a profoundly self-centered worldview. This self-centered perspective is the very root of suffering. To end our suffering, we must completely surrender this perspective. When the addict humbly and honestly asks for divine assistance, it will be granted. When the addict can say, *yet not as I will, but as you will* (Mark 26:39), the result can be miraculous.

Deprivation Addiction

To avoid becoming a dry drunk, an essential part of the healing process for all addicts is to learn appropriate forms of self-nurturance. The underlying addiction in all substance addictions is the addiction to self-deprivation. Self-deprivation of ordinary pleasures is the refusal to self-nurture, the wish to control, and the need to feel separate and superior. The deprivation addict gets a kind of high from not needing ordinary human comforts that everyone else seems to need. Pleasure comes to the deprivation addict not from the natural fulfillment of ordinary human needs but from depriving themselves of fulfillment. In a perverse manner, the deprivation addict may enjoy self-denial more than self-fulfillment. For example, to the deprivation addict not eating when hungry brings more satisfaction and ego gratification than eating does. The deprivation addict feels superior to others who seem to require reasonable amounts of food, rest, play, sex, friendship and so forth. Understanding deprivation addiction helps us realize how many events in life that may seem inexplicable using normal ways of reasoning become more understandable when we realize that self-indulgence and self-deprivation are simply two sides of the same coin.

What Does Addiction Have to Do with Me?

Surrendering self and letting go of the illusion that we are in control frees all of us. It appears to me that we are all addicted to something. Recognizing that fact makes it easier to have compassion for those who are struggling with substance and behavioral addictions.

The refrain of an unpublished song I once wrote called *Blues for Everyone* sums up many of the qualities that make addictive thinking so painful and frustrating:

> *You just want what you want*
> *And you want what you want*
> *When you want it.*

All of us firmly believe we deserve to get what we want, and to get it when we want it. We identify deeply with our self-identity; the historic, conditioned, and programmed *I* that we assume ourselves to be. This comes from our long-held but false programmed beliefs we will go to extraordinary lengths to support and defend.

From the perspective of our ordinary, self-centered thinking and perceiving, we believe the world is full of lack and want. We also believe we are full of lack and want. Children are often programmed to believe that they are inadequate as they are and must be improved by heroic effort or purchasing special products. We are culturally programmed to believe that we can feed our desires and fix our perceived inadequacies. This programming is so automatic and powerful that many people rarely question these beliefs. We need to become deeply aware of our own programming. Careful observation of the content of our minds sets in motion a process of change that results in our behavior becoming less automatic, conditioned and reactive.

Understanding Addictions

Substance and behavioral addictions create enormous pain and suffering for addicts and their families, their employers, and their friends. The work of Dr. David Hawkins is very helpful in understanding addictive thinking patterns. Anyone coping with addiction will benefit from his writings. Dr. Hawkins' scale of consciousness has revealed original and useful ways of understanding human behavior. His intimate familiarity with addictions and spiritual awakening, along with a rare gift for teaching these difficult to understand subjects, is a blessing for us all. It was while reading Dr. Hawkins seminal work *Power vs. Force: The hidden determinants of human behavior (2002)* that I experienced the abiding shift in awareness in 2002.

I have also benefitted from the perceptive writings of Doug Thorburn, who wrote the illuminating book *Drunks, Drugs & Debits: How to Recognize Addicts and Avoid Financial Abuse* (2001). As an aside, I apparently bought the first copy of this book according to a personal note from the author! His books and website have become a large and important contribution to helping victims of hidden addiction. He developed a simple, 20-item scale available online that anyone can use to help recognize subtle signs of addictive behavior in others, including spouses, children, employers, employees, professionals, friends, and so forth. Merely reading these questions will start the reader thinking about behaviors they may have noticed in a hidden addict but never understood. It can be found at www.preventragedy.com.

His books are revealing and informative, and are a must read for anyone involved in either personal or business dealings with someone who may be an addict. Thorburn helps naïve non-addicts recognize the addicts who are in denial about their addiction with whom the non-addict may have daily interaction. He encourages a firm, tough-love approach, which seems to be the perfect antidote to the typical codependent's enabling attempts to help. These frustrating and ultimately futile efforts usually just make a bad situation even worse. Until we understand the nature of addiction, most efforts to aid addicts will backfire. Learning to protect yourself from abuse by those in the throes of addiction is highly recommended. Developing effective means of coping with addictions is of tremendous importance. Learning to recognize addicts who are in denial with whom we interact daily is essential for our own well-being.

Bill W.'s Death and Rebirth

It's instructive to read Bill W.'s description in the *AA Grapevine*, July 1992, of his death *to* the self and rebirth *in* the Self: *I was the recipient in 1934 of a tremendous mystic experience or 'illumination'*. Like Bill, many active addicts are literally dying from their disease. If, like Bill, the active addict commits to the core tenets of AA and surrenders the illusion of self-control by accepting the First Step, they open the way to experience a genuine spiritual rebirth. In the experience of this spiritual rebirth, the addict not only sets them self free, but by surrendering the ego, saves their own life. Once I understood the pivotal importance of being reborn in the spirit, I inquired into how my clients with a history of addiction became sober. They would usually report some experience which was so horrifying that it convinced them of the critical importance of sobriety. Often these experiences involved a profound sense of shame as they violated their own most important values. For others it was being confronted with an inescapable external boundary, such as the second, or fifth DWI. What was truly interesting was how many of these reports involved a real spiritual rebirth. These deeply meaningful and highly personal experiences were not reported until asked.

This rebirth is the real healing from addiction. Without it, relapse into substance abuse is an ever-present danger. Spiritual rebirth can be seen in the context of the Christian experience but can occur outside of a Christian perspective and interpretation as well. Alcoholics Anonymous was developed initially in the United States, where there is a long history of identification with Christianity. The concepts and language of Christianity are found throughout the AA Big Book. While I am very comfortable with this language, at least since the shift in consciousness in 2002, many others are put off by the idea of surrendering to a Higher Power. Because my clients represented a variety of faith and nonfaith backgrounds, I have tried to be radically inclusive in my language and description of the central tenets of a liberated way of life. I am most familiar with Christian and Zen Buddhist concepts and use these liberally and often interchangeably, but awareness is not confined by any set of beliefs.

Is Religious Faith Necessary to be Reborn in the Spirit?

Spiritual rebirth does not depend on or require religious belief. Even the word *spiritual* is superfluous, but we must use language in some manner. Try to resist being thrown off by any words. Remember, when seen clearly and deeply, all beliefs are recognized as ultimately false. Rebirth can refer to almost any experience that appears to have had a transformative effect on the individual. If we experience a genuine rebirth in the Spirit as Jesus Christ describes, all specific denominational beliefs are transcended. With this rebirth, we have no further interest in specific beliefs because we know reality as it is and accept it fully. At the same time, for me personally, this rebirth allowed me to finally understand the profound truth of the teachings of Jesus Christ as I seemed to intuitively understand inner meanings in the Bible that had previously made little sense to me. Consequently, genuine, heartfelt and unwavering faith in the deep truth of Christianity was kindled.

Narcissism

When examining the thinking patterns of addicts, note the extreme narcissism: everything bad that happens is someone else's fault. Active addicts demonstrate extremely narcissistic and irresponsible behaviors. They accept no responsibility for any harm their behavior may cause others, but rather project that responsibility onto someone or something else. When addicts in recovery work through the twelve steps under the guidance of a wise sponsor, they learn to take responsibility for their actions. Amends are made to those harmed where appropriate and helpful. This work is an important and beneficial key in the addict's recovery process.

As I have developed a deeper understanding of narcissism, I have come to see aspects of narcissistic thinking and behavior everywhere. Narcissism does not require substance addiction, but it appears to be universally present when there is an active addiction. Narcissistic thinking patterns can continue indefinitely after sobriety if relentless self-examination, usually with outside assistance, is not pursued indefinitely. We are all incredibly self-centered. In our culture we are programmed to believe that it's appropriate, even healthy, to be self-centered. This self-centered approach is rooted in the belief in a separate, unique, enduring, autonomous self-identity that is nurtured by the thinking mind.

The firm, unquestioning belief in an imaginary internal entity called *me* is the root of suffering. Most of our life is an unending effort to get more of what *I* want and to avoid as much as possible what *I* do not want. We are on a never-ending merry-go-round of craving and desire on the one hand and avoidance and aversion on the other. It is easy to understand why substance and behavioral addictions are so common. Freedom comes only from a radical dissolution of the fantasies that maintain this meaningless, endless, and fruitless pursuit of more, More, MORE.

We are all trying to get what we believe we want and avoid what we don't want, and in this sense we're all addicts. To be certain, this realization doesn't dilute or minimize the trauma of genuine substance or behavioral addictions. Rather, it reveals that addicts and non-addicts alike are all far more similar in basic ways than we may have imagined. None of us transcend the human condition.

This book has presented the process of spiritual awakening and has offered continuous encouragement to practice methods of increasing self-awareness. These practices will help relieve chronic dissatisfaction and will guide in the gradual unfolding of the Self. Paying deliberate attention to our moment-to-moment experience helps us develop our ability to self-nurture. Self-nurturance is not narcissistic. Rather it is a necessary tool in healthy living that provides us with what we need for physical, spiritual and emotional health. Learning to self-nurture develops critical skills that help the addict begin their journey towards recovery. We all could benefit from becoming aware of the teachings of Alcoholics Anonymous, and from reducing the perceived sense of separation from those whose lives seem out of control for any reason. To quote the great American psychiatrist Harry Stack Sullivan, *We are all much more simply human than otherwise* (1966), p.7. Loving kindness towards our self and others, along with firm boundaries when needed, is to be one with the Way.

Chapter Thirteen

RAINBOW'S END

*Underneath your feet
Lies the end of the rainbow
Where else could it be?*

Dog Whisperer Needed: An Example of Non-Doing

One Sunday morning I had the urge to take a drive near my home in the beautiful countryside of upstate New York. A friend and I had several free hours and drove south into Pennsylvania, where many old dairy farms have returned to their natural state prior to cultivation. After driving for a while in the country, we arrived at a small, peaceful lake. If I had a destination in mind, this would be it.

After visiting the lake, we began to slowly meander back north. A few miles up the narrow country road, we were startled to see a large dog attacking a jogger. The dog had leapt the decrepit fence surrounding the farm where it lived and had a firm grip on the jogger's thigh. We could see blood and the jogger's shock and fear. The dog, a Rottweiler, was all focus and intent. Attack was in its genes. Letting go was not.

A hundred yards or so up the hill on the other side of the fence, a middle-aged woman was yelling and pleading fruitlessly for the dog to come back. I have watched enough Cesar Millan *Dog Whisperer* videos to know she couldn't control the dog in mid attack with her yelling. She had to know this also. I believe that perhaps her yelling was so we would know she had tried to subdue the animal, and therefore would not hold her accountable for her dog's out-of-control behavior. The jogger was quickly losing his fight to stay upright. I could sense the energy draining from him, and in a few more seconds he almost certainly would have been on the ground.

I pulled my car right up to the dog and jogger, both of whom were on the edge of the road. I set a brief mental intention that the dog should leave, and within a split second it bounded back over the fence and up the hill from whence it had come.

Even though I am not a dog expert, I know that an attacking Rottweiler is not likely to release its prey. Far more likely, the dog would have attacked even more ferociously once the man was down. The outcome would not have been good for the man or the dog. However, in setting the mental intention, I remained fully in the present moment, focusing my entire intention on the dog releasing its grip from the jogger's leg and returning to its home.

Shortly after I had stopped in one lane, a man driving in the other lane also stopped to help. He had his cell phone out, offering to call police or take the jogger to a hospital. He was clearly eager to help, walking over to the injured runner and assisting him into his car. I realized that I had done my job, that all was OK, that it was time to leave, and so I did.

My friend and I both immediately recognized the experience as a beautiful example of *non-doing*, of Mind operating freely in the world. In this experience with the dog and the jogger, I did not do anything. I just showed up. I did not analyze what I did, how I did it, when I did it, or even if what I did made a difference. I just showed up, followed the guidance I was given to set the mental intention and let the rest unfold according to universal design. I remained in the present moment, focused only on the mental intention I had set.

While I cannot know for sure, it seems like I am inserted into such situations deliberately, although I realize this stretches credulity for some. I say this because I do not remember these events occurring before 2002, although probably they did occur, and I just did not notice. Certainly, they were more subtle, and involved less drama. Now I immediately recognize them for what they are: namely, divine gifts to help me remember the continuous presence of God in the world, and opportunities to act decisively and effectively as an instrument of God's will. I attribute their increased frequency in my life to my absolute surrender to the will of God immediately after my awakening. At least that is when I became fully conscious of my intent to surrender my will completely.

Notice that I take no credit for my actions in this example. I do not deserve credit or blame since I am being used as an instrument by the will of God. In every similar circumstance I recall, my actions were pivotal and certainly exerted a beneficial effect on the situation. My sense is that I am not capable of acting so effortlessly, fearlessly, and skillfully by myself. I need to embody the strength and power of the Holy Spirit to act in this way. It is hard for us to conceive of such an intimate presence in our daily life, yet in Luke 12:6-7 we learn:

> *Are not five sparrows sold for two pennies? Yet not one of them is forgotten by God. Indeed, the very hairs of your head are all numbered. Don't be afraid; you are worth more than many sparrows.*

To live in this way is to see the sacred in all things, making your life an offering to God, a living sacrament.

An infinite number of variables are involved in any act, yet some higher power always knows exactly what we need and what is perfect for the greater good at any given moment.

Life becomes a fascinating adventure when we learn to recognize and dwell continuously in this unnameable, indescribable *something*. In Christian terms, it is known as *the presence of God*. In Buddhist terms it is known as *suchness, Mind,* or *no-mind*. In non-spiritual, nonreligious terms, it is called *reality, presence awareness, things as they are,* and *just this as it is* with nothing added or subtracted. We spend our entire lives trying to know the elusive *this*. Our momentary experiences of direct awareness feed and nurture us, as we long to return to our source, our true home. The practice of presence awareness guides us always on that road.

As we lose interest in our own mind and its endless stream of self-centered, greedy, conditioned thoughts, beliefs, and convictions, we will also lose interest in the approval or disapproval of others. Trying to control and manipulate other people's reactions to us serves no useful purpose and is impossible to accomplish. Intuitively understanding this truth sets us free from the illusion that we can control others, control circumstances and control outcomes. In experiencing this freedom, we at last find our true home. Then the truth of Hakuin Zenji's *Chant in Praise of Zazen* (*Daily Chants and Recitations*, 2005, p. 35) is revealed:

> *This earth where we stand is the pure lotus land,*
> *and this very body the body of Buddha.*

Perception Is All

How we perceive people and events determines our reactions to them. Our perceptions determine the thoughts we have, our interpretation of events, our emotional reactions to our experiences, and our reactions to other people. It is important to realize that we are all inherently perfect, just as we are. Nothing needs to change. We are already whole and complete, just as we are right now. At the same time, to recognize and manifest our true nature requires knowledge and discernment, along with determined and skillful effort. Everything about this path can seem paradoxical, as seemingly opposite truths need to be held simultaneously. It is also true that we have become remarkably adept at forgetting our always-present true nature. We need to continue the practice of noticing and trusting the direct manifestations of the subtle, underlying source that guides and sustains our life.

Returning Home

The rainbow ends where it begins, which is right here, right now. In an important sense, the spiritual journey is about coming home, which is found in the truth that home never left us. Home is always within us. Our conditioned mind leads us to believe we are alone in the world, separate from our source. Until we grasp that we can never lose the ground of our being, we will *endlessly wander, poor on this earth* (Hakuin Zenji, p. 22, op. cit.). Unlike Dorothy in the iconic movie *The Wizard of Oz*, we do not need a magic spell to awake from our slumber. All we need is to recognize this central truth, that home has been with us all along. It could never be anywhere else.

In his poem *A Spiritual Journey* (1987), Wendell Berry notes that we discover the world not by ordinary searching, but by a difficult search which ends at our own feet. We must struggle mightily for spiritual realization, while simultaneously realizing our own efforts will never be enough. St. Augustine acknowledges this peculiar truth when he notes the importance of personal striving for union with the Creator. While personal effort appears to be necessary, it can never be enough. Some other force, subtle and mysterious, must somehow take us through the final dissolution.

Amazing Grace

The self-identity cannot transcend itself. Our own efforts, though critical, can take us only so far. It is important to understand as we approach this leap into the unknown that nothing can ever be lost, and nothing needs to be found. The void is not empty.

Absolute, abject surrender is necessary to take the final plunge into no-mind awareness. This surrender has both a voluntary and an involuntary component. The self-identity or thinking mind must be willing at a deep level to let go and trust in what is. This level of surrender is a prerequisite to the disappearance of the self-identity. Only Divine Guidance makes this possible, for we can never disappear to this extent by our own efforts.

A wonderful example of this is found in the moving hymn *Amazing Grace*, wherein the composer John Newton speaks of being lost. By grace he awakens to what is real. He could not achieve this release on his own. Neither can we. It is all the result of unfathomable grace.

The Prodigal Son

Consider the beautiful and deeply instructive story of the Prodigal Son Jesus shares in the Gospel of Luke, 15:11–32:

> *[11] Jesus continued: There was a man who had two sons. [12] The younger one said to his father, 'Father, give me my share of the estate.' So he divided his property between them.*
>
> *[13] Not long after that, the younger son got together all he had, set off for a distant country and there squandered his wealth in wild living. [14] After he had spent everything, there was a severe famine in that whole country, and he began to be in need. [15] So he went and hired himself out to a citizen of that country, who sent him to his*

fields to feed pigs. ¹⁶He longed to fill his stomach with the pods that the pigs were eating, but no one gave him anything.

¹⁷When he came to his senses, he said, 'How many of my father's hired servants have food to spare, and here I am starving to death! ¹⁸I will set out and go back to my father and say to him: Father, I have sinned against heaven and against you. ¹⁹I am no longer worthy to be called your son; make me like one of your hired servants. ²⁰So he got up and went to his father.

But while he was still a long way off, his father saw him and was filled with compassion for him; he ran to his son, threw his arms around him and kissed him.

²¹ The son said to him, 'Father, I have sinned against heaven and against you. I am no longer worthy to be called your son.'

²² But the father said to his servants, 'Quick! Bring the best robe and put it on him. Put a ring on his finger and sandals on his feet ²³Bring the fattened calf and kill it. Let's have a feast and celebrate. ²⁴For this son of mine was dead and is alive again; he was lost and is found.' So they began to celebrate.

²⁵ Meanwhile, the older son was in the field. When he came near the house, he heard music and dancing. ²⁶So he called one of the servants and asked him what was going on. ²⁷'Your brother has come,' he replied, 'and your father has killed the fattened calf because he has him back safe and sound.'

²⁸The older brother became angry and refused to go in. So his father went out and pleaded with him. ²⁹But he answered his father, 'Look! All these years I've been slaving for you and never disobeyed your orders. Yet you never gave me even a young goat so I could celebrate with my friends. ³⁰But when this son of yours who has squandered your property with prostitutes comes home, you kill the fattened calf for him!'

³¹ 'My son,' the father said, 'you are always with me, and everything I have is yours. ³²But we had to celebrate and be glad,

because this brother of yours was dead and is alive again; he was lost and is found.'

This story is profound with a lot more to it than meets the eye. The conventional interpretation is obvious; the lost son faces reality and recognizes that he has made a horrible mess of things. He lets reality into his fantasy world of wine, women, and song. In so doing, he gives up, surrenders completely.

I wonder, though, if this story could convey an even more radical truth. The following deeper meaning was revealed to me through no-mind awareness. In Luke 15:20, we find that our erstwhile, tattered, bedraggled, profligate explorer got up and went to his father. But while he was still a long way off, his father saw him and was filled with compassion for him. What does his father *see*?

After their loving reunion, the father orders a great feast to be prepared, gives the son his best robe, a ring, and new sandals. The father's joy knows no bounds. *For this son of mine was dead and is alive again; he was lost and is found.* What are we to make of this? After enormous self-indulgence and the resulting profound disappointment and despair, the younger brother *came to his senses*; he wakes up to reality. Awakening is about becoming able to see things as they are, rather than as we wish they were, fear they might be, or believe they should be. He wakes up, and thus the father can't contain his joy.

It is important to recognize that the father is a deeply awakened man, able to see clearly through the eye of wisdom. For such a man, nothing could be more wonderful than to have his son recognize, for himself, the truth of who and what he is. His son returns to his true home, having finally recognized the futility of searching in foreign lands for what was always right in front of him all the time. The father's own realization and resulting energetic attunement make this profound change evident to him long before his son is within his line of sight. The father instantly recognizes that the one who came home is not the one who left. The father was fully awake and thus could recognize the awakened presence in his returning son.

This recognition brought the father infinite joy as his lost son died to his previous understanding of who he was. The no longer lost son can now begin the process of learning to live, as clear vision will guide him now. Instead of his previous dependence on conditioned beliefs about reality, he will be able to discern what is true for himself. It is analogous to the birth of a baby who rapidly blinks after birth while his or her eyes adjust to the bright light of this new world. Once the baby's vision is clear, he or she begins the journey forward, making new discoveries about themselves every day. So, too, it is with the lost son. While he is not yet fully awake, his vision still partially occluded as he still struggles with self-judgment and guilt, a fundamental shift *has* occurred.

The metaphor of the prodigal son reveals an important truth about the dutiful older brother. He is understandably perplexed and becomes angry, refusing to join in the festivities. This grand celebration honoring the return of the lost son makes no sense to him and does not seem fair. The father, fruitlessly, tries to help him see why his joy is so great: *My son, you're always with me, and everything I have is yours* (Luke 15:31).

The prodigal son had looked to others to nourish his hunger, but no one could have given him what he really needed. The prodigal son needed a shift in consciousness and had to be willing to surrender his old beliefs and assumptions for that to occur. He had to be willing to surrender everything he thought to be true. Until reaching a pivotal moment of complete hopelessness, he believed that through his own efforts he could have all that he craved. The older son, who remained loyally behind with his father, firmly believed that following the rules and being good in a conventional sense would suffice to grant him entrance into the kingdom of heaven. Far from it. He had to become a different being to enter the new covenant taught by Jesus Christ.

This is a realization we must all come to for ourselves. The most a genuine teacher can do is to speak the truth clearly and demonstrate awakened awareness through acting freely in the ordinary world of daily life. The story of the Prodigal Son is a beautiful example of the transformation that can occur in anyone through unfathomable grace when we involuntarily, absolutely, and totally give up our wish to control our life. The struggle to see things as they really are is a struggle we all experience alone. Only when we surrender all our preconceived notions can this unfathomable grace permeate and move freely through us.

Dutiful Is Not Enough

One of the primary missions of Jesus' teaching was to deconstruct the notion that observing the myriad rules and regulations of Jewish law would unlock the door to God's grace. Many of the stories in the Gospels describe Jesus routinely ignoring these man-made laws and adhering to the higher laws of the Father. For example, one man-made law during Jesus' time ruled that it was a capital offense to heal the sick on the Sabbath. Jesus ignored this law and healed on the Sabbath, because the law of his Father took precedence. What Jesus teaches is radical and destabilizing to the religious order of his time. Jesus throws into chaos the easy to believe construct that obedience to man-made laws is enough to practice the spiritual life. His teaching challenges all to think outside the box of man-made laws, to reflect on whether these laws help and heal or hinder and hurt all the people of God. Obsessional obedience to rules is not enough. It does, however, engender enormous spiritual pride.

Jesus' teaching is radical and destabilizing because it is impossible to grasp with our thinking mind. Black and white thinking and rigid subservience to man-made rules of behavior was never enough to enter the Kingdom of God. We must become one with this truth, moving beyond an intellectual understanding of it, so that it becomes our truth; a truth we hold deep within our being.

After his great awakening Shakyamuni Buddha saw the problem Jesus faced. For an extended period, he refused to teach, believing that this *Dharma* (true teaching) was so subtle, that no one would ever understand it. Even today, teaching what is real is a challenging endeavor when compared to teaching what is familiar, safe and comfortable.

Jesus was crucified for simply telling the truth, but he could not do anything else. When asked directly by the Sanhedrin High Priest, he cannot deny who he is. Luke 22:70: *So they all asked, "Are You then the Son of God?" He replied, "You say that I am."* To be one with this truth is a solitary and difficult journey indeed.

The Prodigal Son's father saw immediately, even from a great distance, that his son who had been lost was now found. In other words, his son was now waking up to the truth of what was so, and as such could then begin his journey toward full awakening.

Most spiritual quests are messy and confusing. Those who are content with a conventional life often judge harshly those who seek a deeper truth. This judgment comes from a place of fear. Those who are content with where they are on their own journey cherish order, structure, and predictability. In the story of the Prodigal Son, the older brother had been content in his journey. The return home of the Prodigal and the life lesson the older brother learned from his father's complete acceptance of the Prodigal, drives the older brother to keep searching. He no longer is content to stay stuck in his conventional understanding, and so his new spiritual journey begins.

Comfort is not our companion on this journey. If we are seriously committed to spiritual growth and desire walking with Jesus, Shakyamuni Buddha, Abraham, Moses, Krishna, and other enlightened ones, we need to do what we can through our own efforts. Since this path is so challenging and uncertain, we must somehow find enormous courage to push forward without knowing for sure where the road will lead. The difficulty is real. The miracle is that each of us has everything we need to reach our true home.

All we must do is begin.

Chapter Fourteen

MY JOURNEY HOME

Days Turn into Years: Becoming a Psychologist

After graduation from high school, I attended Vanderbilt University along with half of my (small) high school graduating class. During my senior year, I had read an article in *Newsweek* about a clinical psychologist in New York City who was in the self-employed private practice of psychotherapy. I knew immediately that this was what I also wanted to do in my professional life. I wrote him a letter, asking him what I should do in college to be able to attend graduate school in clinical psychology. To my astonishment, he replied in detail. I then proceeded to do exactly what he recommended.

In college I majored in psychology with a marked interest in literature, philosophy, and religion. A turning point in my academic career occurred at the end of the first semester of my junior year. Two days before a final exam in Abnormal Psychology, I carelessly rammed my mint 1961 Volkswagen Beetle into a telephone pole. Imported from Germany, it had none of the safety gear required for American cars. Without Plexiglas, the windshield shattered into a million pieces upon impact, showering a friend and me with tiny glass missiles. I was driving him home late at night and fell asleep at the wheel. Miraculously, we both emerged relatively unscathed. I received a broken nose from the experience, which a doctor at the local emergency room refused to fix.

I went in to explain to my Abnormal Psychology professor why I would have to delay taking his final exam. My nose was still broken and shoved about half an inch to the left of where it should have been. Dr. Robert Liebert listened without much comment and then informed me that I would have to take the exam as scheduled or fail the course. We then spent the better part of an hour arguing respectfully and discussing the merits of our respective positions.

He won. However, possibly he saw something in me he liked (Tenacious? Bright? Argumentative? Goal-oriented? Obnoxious?). He graciously suggested I do research in his lab, working closely with his doctoral graduate students. I accepted somewhat grudgingly, having no idea how valuable such experience would be in graduate school applications. The next three semesters I diligently worked for Dr. Liebert and his graduate students. One result was a very strong letter of reference. A second outcome of this work was a research publication. Both helped immeasurably in gaining admission and financial support at several top graduate programs in clinical psychology. I am still grateful. Thanks Dr. Liebert.

Another key influence at Vanderbilt was a wonderful professor of religion named Winston King. Dr. King taught courses in the history, philosophy, and phenomenology of religion at the Vanderbilt Divinity School as well as in the graduate and undergraduate Department of Religion. He had visited Southeast Asia and written a book about his experiences with meditation called *A Thousand Lives Away: Buddhism in Contemporary Burma* (1962). Dr. King allowed me to forego the required prerequisites to take his graduate course in the phenomenology of religion and a course in the philosophy of religion.

During my senior year at Vanderbilt, I had the remarkable opportunity to meet Shibayama *Roshi*, probably the most highly respected Japanese Zen master alive at that time. Roshi is a Japanese term that refers to highly esteemed, widely experienced, and older Zen masters. Dr. King had been instrumental in bringing Shibayama Roshi to Nashville. This tiny man (well under 5 feet) and his even smaller female translator showed up for a meeting with students in my dormitory, of all places. After speaking briefly in Japanese, he asked if there were any questions. No one knew what to say, so I spoke up. *How do you begin to study Zen?* I asked Shibayama Roshi. Through his interpreter, he simply stated, *Learn to sit.* I had just read the recently released *Three Pillars of Zen* (1967) by my future Zen teacher Roshi Phillip Kapleau, so this answer made some sense to me. No one can say why some experiences cut so deeply but reading Roshi Kapleau's book and then meeting an authentic Zen master in the flesh, a real rarity at that time, propelled me onto the path that became my life's purpose.

After graduating from Vanderbilt, I attended the graduate program in clinical psychology at Indiana University in Bloomington, Indiana. The further I went in formal academic training, the better were my interest and performance. Having progressively more opportunity to do the kind of work that I liked was highly motivating. Graduating with a PhD in clinical psychology, I briefly considered an academic or research position at a major university. However, my career goal had always been clinical service work.

I completed the required yearlong clinical internship to become a clinical psychologist at the National Institutes of Mental Health in Washington, DC. I had then satisfied the formal requirements for licensure as a professional psychologist. However, I loved being a student in my field of study, so I applied for a two-year postdoctoral fellowship in the Department of Psychiatry at the University of Rochester School of Medicine and Dentistry. This position provided the best possible training available. A side benefit was the nearby Rochester Zen Center. During this two-year (1973-75) postdoctoral fellowship at the University of Rochester Medical Center, my wife and I lived only a few blocks from the Rochester Zen Center. Daily walks past the Zen Center were part of my exercise routine. Strangely, I could not bring myself to go inside or even knock on the door! It was too intimidating, too foreign, and yet completely fascinating. A deep attraction to and simultaneous fear of the Zen Center arose. This approach-avoidance conflict is probably typical of someone who is seriously considering whether to begin spiritual practice. As I had read and reread *The Three Pillars of Zen*, the self-identity knew that trouble lay ahead!

As much as I wished to begin training at the Zen Center, I had tremendous fear. Chronic physical and emotional tension, along with fear of losing control, led to paralysis. In retrospect, probably the time just was not right. Immersion in the quest for self-transcendence cannot be forced. There must be a deep readiness. It happens in God's time.

It eventually became clear that everything happens exactly as it should. No accidents occur anywhere. Anything that occurs needs to occur. Why? Because it did. There's no other reason. All is well, always, whether we can see it that way or not. Eventually we recognize that everything is perfect. Nothing needs to be any different. This is not a belief, but rather a spontaneous realization out of what I now call no mind awareness. Beliefs are largely if not completely useless, even harmful. This is because all beliefs come from and reinforce the primacy of our own thinking mind. Eventually all beliefs must be surrendered.

These truths may sound something like New Age mumbo jumbo. In the past when I heard similar statements, I felt a strong temptation to write them off as revealing a lack of intellectual rigor and denial of personal responsibility. However, from the perspective of awakened awareness, everything really is perfect, just being itself, exactly the way it is.

It was only after moving away from Rochester in 1975 that I was able to practice Zen Buddhism. Through a remarkable serendipity, I saw a small notice on an out of the way bulletin board at Binghamton University where I worked describing a zazen group. Zazen is the form of meditation favored in the Zen tradition. The contact person turned out to be a professor of psychology and a very dedicated Zen practitioner. I feel a debt of gratitude to him, as he was the first in what would later prove to be a long line of truly committed spiritual seekers who assisted me. I began to sit with the group he had formed three times a week for two hours at a time.

Meditation and More

One of the first things I noticed when doing this silent meditation was how angry I was. Every time I sat on the mat and faced myself, only because there was no other choice, I would become aware of this anger. I had not consciously noticed this anger before and would have denied it if asked. However, stuck on a meditation cushion with nowhere to go and nothing else to do, I was forced to acknowledge the truth. I was a chronically angry person. Interestingly, the anger had no content. I was not angry about anything I could identify, but I was angry. Every time I sat with the meditation group the experience was the same. It would take a solid hour of dedicated silent meditation before the anger would dissipate. The interesting thing was that it did finally release and did so every time. It did not release because I made a deliberate and successful effort to release it. It released because I did nothing whatsoever except allow it to be, exactly as it was. Just this, nothing added or subtracted. My meditation practice at the time was a very basic breath meditation of counting inhalations and exhalations from one to ten, then beginning again at one. When I lost track of the count, I would return once again to one.

Stress-related emotional and physical problems were routine for me at the time. During the first experience of sitting meditation, a lump in the throat that would not go away disappeared. Diagnosed with pre-hypertension at the age of 28, I was told by a cardiologist that I would need medication if I did not get my blood pressure down. For the previous several years, panic attacks had been frighteningly persistent. We understood very little about panic disorder at the time. Several phobias developed, including fears of being up high, driving over bridges, and riding in elevators. Flying in airplanes and riding buses could at times precipitate feelings of panic. I avoided these situations whenever possible.

Regular zazen began without any expectation. However, all the stress-related symptoms gradually faded and mostly disappeared. Walking through the mall one day, I stopped to take my blood pressure at one of the machines that were available to the public for seventy-five cents. The reading was 110/70. This was startling, as the numbers routinely had been 140/90 in a wide variety of situations. Over the next month, repeated readings on that machine and numerous others confirmed the readings were even lower. Frequently the numbers would be 100/60 or less. Being still somewhat of a worrier, I then wondered if I could go too low. Reading up on it led to a decision to ignore the numbers and just live life. It was years later before I attributed the change in blood pressure to the six hours a week of zazen.

Seeing Clearly

In my apartment one night in January 1982, I opened the *Three Pillars of Zen* (Kapleau, 1980, p. 374) and read these stunning lines from *The Heart Sutra*, a classic Zen Buddhist text: *Form here is only emptiness; emptiness only form.* After reading these lines, I went to bed and lay in the dark. A visual image appeared before my eyes that I knew was me. I saw myself as a tiny being composed of infinite points of colored light. Simultaneously, I realized that I held myself together by intention and will. I realized that if I stopped actively holding myself together, I would disappear. I had a moment of real terror, as I recognized the possibility of total dissolution. At that moment, Roshi

Kapleau's face appeared. He said in a calm voice, *You can't fall out of the universe.* Somewhat inexplicably, this was exactly what I needed to hear.

Some level of stark terror typically arises at the moment of the ego's letting go of its death grip on delusion. This was my opportunity to freak out. In the next instant, however, I released the energetic constriction that had been holding *me* together, and the tiny dots of light flew apart in every direction, disappearing. What was left? Nothing…. emptiness…. the Void. Yet this empty void was in some way full, scintillating, alive, ecstatic. The void was dark, but also lit by some ineffable light. Fear was gone completely. From that moment until some indeterminate period had passed, the *I* was completely gone. The self-identity creates the sense of separation we normally experience. Now there was no sense of separation with all that is. There was neither a body nor a mind, and yet awareness continued. This empty, unitive awareness in which there is no subject or object is our true nature. It is who we are before we are born, while we are alive, and after we die. It is unchanging, cannot be affected by any experiences, and does not become more or less. These conceptual statements represent the post-experience attempt to express coherently the ineffable and unnameable. Such thoughts were not present during the experience.

The overall lighting in the room was dark, yet I could see clearly. All objects were ephemeral, transparent, or translucent. I could see infinite stars in the heavens. Although there was darkness everywhere, the darkness was somehow simultaneously illuminated. This *seeing* seemed strange only in retrospect, as I never left my bed during this experience and could see only the ceiling with my normal vision. The emotional experience was pure joy, like nothing ever experienced. I had no thought or self-awareness, just awareness experiencing itself. It is impossible to describe. We are never the same afterwards. Such an experience is just a brief taste of our unconditioned awareness, which is never absent, yet rarely is experienced or noticed.

The next morning, normal awareness returned, bringing along with it very vulnerable and ungrounded feelings. I called the Rochester Zen Center and asked to speak with someone who could help me understand the experience. Bodhin, who is now Bodhin Roshi and the spiritual director of the Rochester Zen Center, was then a Zen priest and monk. The receptionist summoned Bodhin and he quickly got on the phone. Bodhin was a familiar figure because I had attended several one-day introductory workshops at the Zen Center. On the phone, he was very calming and reassuring. Bodhin suggested coming to a workshop at the Zen Center and consulting with Roshi Kapleau about the experience. Several months later, this meeting occurred.

Roshi Kapleau described the experience as genuine, but not deep enough to be *kensho*. *Literally, kensho means 'seeing into one's own nature'* (Kapleau, P., p. 369). Experientially, kensho involves a radical upheaval in the very ground of one's being. This new way of being must be demonstrated behaviorally by speaking and acting out of no-mind awareness. Roshi compared my experience to a crack in the Plexiglas, but not a hole right through it. In this context, Plexiglas refers to the subtle but powerful buffer erected by our concepts, beliefs, and assumptions. These mental constructs aren't real, but our blind belief in them comes between us and our direct, unvarnished experience of what *is*. In this first meeting, Roshi Kapleau mentioned casually that perhaps I would start and lead a Zen meditation group in Binghamton. I never forgot his gentle suggestion.

Zen Training

Roshi Kapleau encouraged my attendance at *sesshin*, the intensive Zen retreats that I had so far avoided. I followed his advice, beginning with a couple of two-day silent retreats, then several four-day retreats.

All the retreats I did were powerful and meaningful. Each one was unique and different, exposing new layers of my ignorance, lack of mindful attention, and multiple bad habits of thought, feeling and behavior. I loved the extreme physical and emotional challenge of these grueling experiences. There was intense physical pain as I learned to sit stock still in some version of the lotus posture for more than ten hours a day. It seemed like a form of torture to which I voluntarily submitted. Friends thought I was crazy. I wondered sometimes myself, but attendance was not a choice. Some inner willingness pushed me to continue onward. Blindly I grappled with my meditation practice.

The pull of silent retreats was strong and inexplicable. Zen students had a common saying to reassure each other that their efforts were worthwhile. It was, *The only thing worse than going to sesshin is not going to sesshin.* Maybe something in me knew that I had to do this work in this difficult form. In retrospect, we often can see that life provided us with exactly the right challenges we needed to grow spiritually and emotionally every step of the way.

During prolonged silent meditation, I experienced inner peace and stillness for the first time in a somewhat consistent, predictable manner. Having been chronically anxious for many years, I welcomed this inner quiet. I couldn't identify it at the time, but I now know that there were long periods early on in my retreat experience when my mind simply stopped its ceaseless chatter. This was a tremendous blessing. This inner *stopping* is the goal of all serious spiritual practice. stopping the mind's meaningless but incessant obsessing happens on its own. We can't make ourselves stop thinking.

The endless internal dialogues stop as a natural side effect of total absorption in some focused, intense activity. Any activity that helps us create moments of inner silence will become important in our life. This is a primary reason people become deeply, even compulsively, drawn to many different activities. Something about the activity helps create inner silence and spaciousness. In this inner stillness, creativity and genuine insight flourish. From this mysterious silence, an inner knowing emerges spontaneously. Only later do we put this new awareness into language. The awareness occurs prior to language.

Thinking limits our ability to see and to know directly. Once we have put the awareness into words, we're one step removed from the direct experience itself. Prolonged meditation retreats allow us to learn to experience the world directly without the interpolation of thought. We are addicted to the very thing, thinking, that is the cause of our problems. The only real problem any of us has is the perception of separation. This perception disappears when we experience the world directly without the mediation of thinking.

Just a Taste

Finally, I had proven my resilience and dedication sufficiently to attend a seven-day retreat led by Roshi Kapleau. At the very end of the first seven-day retreat, I had another near-kensho experience.

In the afternoon of the sixth day of this retreat, the bell rang ending a period of sitting meditation. I bolted out of the zendo, across the garden, and up the stairs of the Buddha Hall. This building was where the mandatory yoga class soon would be held. Halfway up the staircase, I snapped back into my ordinary awareness. Startled, I had no idea whether I had clothes on and had to look down at my legs to see if I did. Everything was well until I looked back across the garden and saw no sign of life. There was a complete sense of disorientation. Soon others began to emerge from the meditation hall and move towards me. I could not believe how fast I had moved. Growing up, I often heard that I moved at the speed of molasses. This time it was more like tele transportation. It was as if I had materialized in the stairwell without any effort expended. Many other internal experiences and realizations appeared to accompany this altered awareness of myself.

I had experienced a taste of *wu wei,* a Chinese term meaning action without an actor. I can say this now, although at the time I had no clue what was going on. All I knew was that something had radically changed. My awareness and experience of the world continued to be profoundly altered and far more interesting. Nothing seemed to require any effort, a welcome relief from my usual retreat experience of physical pain and struggle. Every experiential shift in consciousness made the practice easier and more fascinating.

Where Is *Mu*?

That evening I appeared as usual for the private meeting with my teacher, but now with a vast increase in focus and energy. The protocol for such meetings was strict. Opening the door to the room, I would step in, bow, step up to within three feet or so of Roshi Kapleau, and perform three prostrations. I would then sit on a mat directly in front of him in the zazen posture and verbally report my practice.

The initial koan practice is focused on coming to an experiential, nonconceptual understanding of Joshu's *Mu*. This koan is the first case in the Mumonkan compiled by Zen Master Mumon in 1228. Joshu (born 778) was a famous and powerful Chinese Zen (Chan) master. Briefly, in this koan a monk asks Joshu, *Does a dog have the Buddha nature?* Joshu's answer is *Mu*, Chinese for *Nothing*. Joshu's comment throws sand into the gears of the thinking mind and pushes us towards no-mind. The degree of suffering and inner turmoil experienced by Zen students struggling to know Mu directly is the result of loyalty and allegiance to ordinary ways of thinking and perceiving. Like all koans, we initially struggle to grasp this koan with our thinking mind until a deeper practice emerges on its own. This process can take days, months, years, or forever. To realize experientially the truth of a koan requires an internal flip of the mind that we call awakening.

Normally silent during my initial entry into the dokusan (private meeting) room, this evening Roshi began firing questions at me as soon as I entered. *Show me Mu! Where is Mu?! Who is Mu?!* My answers were halting, confused, uncertain. What astounded and impressed me was his ability to see instantly that something had changed radically in me since our last meeting at 6:00 that morning. Before I opened my mouth, he was testing me.

A sage, experienced Zen master sees with the wisdom eye of direct, no-mind awareness having activated intuitive seeing and knowing. He demanded as much from me. There is an old saying, *Practice must be real practice, and awakening must be real awakening.* He encouraged me to not let go of Mu for even a second and to practice even more fervently. Plow ahead! Not knowing where I was going or how to get there, I nevertheless dove in like legions of seekers of the Way before me.

I thought I was close to realization, so I stayed up all night meditating, trying to hold onto my practice with every ounce of strength left in me after six days of relentless zazen with minimal sleep or food. However, staying up all night didn't work either. In retrospect, I believe I was trying to force this inner explosion by sheer will and physical exertion. The ego tried to thrust its way into disappearing, which is impossible.

Intense effort and determination can take you a long way, right to the brink, but not over it. The ego cannot affect its own dissolution. Seeing directly into your true nature typically does require persistent, intense, focused concentration and effort. A fine line exists, though, between pushing too hard and trying to force it, on the one hand, and being too lackadaisical on the other.

During retreats with a Zen master, silence is rigidly enforced. The only exception is during the brief, private one-on-one meetings with the teacher called *dokusan*. The disappointment was crushing when Roshi ended the last dokusan without approving my realization as deep enough to be kensho.

In Zen, the focus is always on a direct, experiential understanding. We cannot convey clearly in words using conceptual thought this experiential understanding. In these private encounters, what we *say* is not enough. A true teacher is interested only in what we *are*. We must demonstrate this realization behaviorally with our whole being. Zen masters require that we are the answer.

An accurate conceptual understanding or description is often worse than useless. Such answers demonstrate that we have not yet even begun to release our death-grip on our delusional self-cherishing. We cannot just talk about it or describe it. We must *be* it. An old saying is, *Those who Know don't say; those who say don't Know.* The *Knowing* described here is the knowing of no-mind, the intuitive awareness of what *is*. This subtle way of knowing arises on its own, spontaneously. Its transmission occurs outside of words and letters.

Kensho

My third seven-day retreat was at the beginning of November in 1984. This retreat occurred immediately after my beloved grandmother died on Halloween day of that year. Determined to attend my grandmother's funeral yet not miss the retreat, I flew to Nashville and then straight to Rochester after the funeral. As the retreat began, I seemed to be able to summon a deeper level of resolve coupled with a calm, quiet focus. I dedicated any merit accrued in the retreat to my grandmother.

Early in the retreat, she appeared before me, seeming lost and confused. This was about five days after her passing. I mentally explained to her that she had died, and it was now time for her to move on. I encouraged her to go to the light, knowing that she would understand what this meant in her current situation. She immediately vanished. I have always believed that she came to me at such a crucial juncture because I was both open and able to help. I was grateful to be of service during her transition, as she had always been infinitely loving and supportive of me.

Having dedicated the retreat to my grandmother, I put my heart and soul into the practice. In the very last dokusan of the seven-day retreat, I entered the private meeting with Roshi Kapleau convinced that I was finally present for what is ultimately real. Roshi had been testing, pushing, pulling, cajoling, and encouraging me throughout the retreat. I was in good hands, and I instinctively knew I could trust this man with my life. We both sensed a change had occurred. Roshi challenged me far more directly and repeatedly than ever before. Some of my answers were still halting, but most were clear, direct, and concise. I was surprised at the answers I heard myself saying forcefully and confidently, without thought.

These answers flew out of my mouth spontaneously, as I repeatedly answered questions without knowing the answers. A strange but electric freedom emerged, as Mu moved, spoke, and demonstrated understanding without a moment's self-reflection or hesitation. I answered six or eight subsequent koans which are normally given after Mu is passed that I had never heard before. By the end of this interaction, Roshi approved my realization after repeated and varied tests were satisfied.

We accomplish nothing on our own. It is the teacher's role to recognize the nondual awareness when it spontaneously emerges. Like a spiritual midwife, a gifted teacher can prompt the further unfolding of the fragile, evanescent glimpse of reality that initially emerges. As student practitioners of the Way, we must be willing to pursue passionately, devotedly, even a whiff of the truth when it arises. It is rare for fully formed and developed awareness to spring from the muck of the thinking mind, yet occasionally it does happen. For all practical purposes, however, we need to assume that for us ordinary mortals, much further work remains after even a genuine and deep awakening emerges.

After kensho, I attended seven-day meditation retreats on a regular basis for four more years. This appears in retrospect to have been a period of integration and deepening of the nondual awareness. It was in many ways a difficult and frustrating time. I was apparently making progress in some manner, but still had no clue what I was doing. I knew I was profoundly different in some indescribable way, yet I was simultaneously painfully aware of how seldom I could manifest this awareness in my daily life. Although I felt fortunate to receive a direct taste of unconditioned awareness, the realization was fleeting, ephemeral. As hard as the I tried, I could not recreate what grace provided. This painful lack of continuous union with *all that is* lasted for fourteen more years and then disappeared in a flash, as described in Chapter 1.

Searching: Not Knowing Why, What or How

Looking back, I would now say that the time from 1988-2002 was a prolonged period of ceaseless searching. I was absolutely compelled to seek, but I had no clue what I was seeking or how to seek it. My formal Zen practice faded and largely disappeared, although in 1998 I did organize and begin to lead a weekly meditation group. The crush of daily life swallowed up most formal practice.

Consciously I had given up on the seemingly grandiose notion of becoming deeply enlightened in this lifetime. Everything I had read implied that such a continuous awakening was virtually unknown in the current era. Even a thousand or more years ago, renowned Zen masters complained about the increasing difficulty of waking up in their "modern" times! Besides, even if such a transformation were possible, it would surely be available only to those who devoted every second of their lives to this pursuit. This would require being a monastic and living in a Zen monastery, something I could not do.

I am describing this period now as if I knew what I was doing. Believe me, I did not. It's only in retrospect that I can make some sense of this relentless and prolonged struggle. I now realize that I had no choice in this passionate seeking. After experiencing the smallest glimpse of Reality, it is impossible to turn one's back on the search to experience again being truly alive. It is out of our hands. Do not worry about it. This searching goes on in a subterranean way, whether we are aware of it or not. We are so fortunate. Something somehow reaches out to guide and sustain us once we commit ourselves fully.

In 1998, sixteen years after Roshi Kapleau's suggestion, I finally had an opportunity to form a meditation group. I invited a small group of friends to meet once a week for an hour of silent sitting together. *Wherever two or more are gathered together...* In this group, I was merely the organizer with no presumption to teach anyone anything. My life involved participating heavily in family life and my psychotherapy practice. Yet this silent, persistent yearning continued on its own, largely outside of conscious awareness.

For several years before 2002 when the last and most enduring shift in consciousness occurred, I traveled the country learning different energetic approaches to relieving psychological suffering. I learned *Thought Field Therapy* from Dr. Roger Callahan, and an offshoot of TFT known as *Emotional Freedom Therapy* (EFT) from its founder,

Gary Craig. I received certification from Dr. Francine Shapiro in *EMDR*.

I also completed Level 2 training in *Touch for Health*, and attended a weeklong intensive course in *Body Talk*, another energetic healing modality taught by John Veltheim. During this course, I met his wife Esther and attended my first *Satsang* with her. Esther was a petite, blonde, attractive English woman who sat before us wearing a T-shirt that said *Rock and Roll Forever* on the front. We are not in Kansas anymore, Dorothy!

Satsang is more common in the Hindu tradition. Many American and European teachers of nondual awareness have chosen some variation of this spontaneous question-and-answer format as a method of teaching well suited to contemporary Western students. Compared to the physically grueling and largely nonverbal Zen tradition, it seemed like a breath of fresh air to me.

Daily Life

In the manner we choose to live our lives, we are mostly deaf, dumb, and blind. We need to recognize and acknowledge this unfortunate truth. There is no need to wonder how we got this way. There is no value in blaming or judging ourselves or anybody else for this. Everyone is doing the same thing. The human condition is universal. Who cares how it started? The bottom line is that none of us escape this life unscathed, yet we all possess the potential to be present in this world in a manner that is enormously beneficial to all beings.

Who knows why anything happens the way it does? As a clinical psychologist, I seek causal explanations for human behavior. With experience, we can become very adroit at fabricating stories about why people act the way they do. At the time, these explanations seem reasonable. Sometimes they are helpful to others. However, with awakening there occurs an almost complete loss of interest in creating stories to explain our behavior. The real reason we acted the way we did is that we acted that way! Why did I make the decisions I made at critical junctures in my life? I do not know. Of course, in retrospect, it is possible to go back and give many reasons why I did what I did in all stages of my life. There can be value in these narratives of our life, but rarely do they reach the root of the problem. Although still deeply curious about understanding people and their behavior, I have less interest in the very limited understanding normally available to our thinking minds.

Our conjectures about why we did what we did are often nothing more than imaginary creations and fantasies. It is best to lose interest in this useless project. By our preoccupation with fantasies and obsessions, we severely limit our ability to see clearly. That is assuming we can see anything at all! When the mind is resting, open, silent, and free, spontaneous realizations of real power and value may emerge, seemingly from nowhere.

Some of the people and experiences who were most valuable to my spiritual and emotional growth appeared to be hurtful or even traumatizing at the time. Our vision is so limited. To say that humility is required for the growth of awareness is a vast understatement. Now I am deeply grateful for everything. It is astounding that one so seemingly thick and stubborn as I was given the grace to *see*.

Becoming Nothing, Really

What has life been like since the continuous awareness mysteriously dawned in 2002? Nothing stays the same, yet the surface of my life remains remarkably undisturbed. Change is the one constant in life. Yet underneath all the activity, always present, is the silence. Utter stillness is our true nature. There is nothing at all that we can say about it. Anything we do say is not quite *it*. Strangely, things continue to happen, but with minimal sense of a *one* doing anything. There is an awareness of rising in the morning, getting dressed, and leaving for work. What is mostly missing is the idea of a *me* that is in charge of this activity. This absence of a personal me creates a wonderful sense of freedom and spontaneity.

Why questions seem like a largely meaningless exercise in futility. Why are people unkind? Why does God allow misfortune to befall the virtuous? Why do I go to work? *I don't know* would be a fully appropriate answer. An equally valid answer to that question might be *Because I do*. Or perhaps a more provocative and abstruse though equally true answer is that *No one goes anywhere or does anything, yet events appear to occur*. Another possible answer would be to stare blankly at the one asking the question! Do we really know for sure why we do anything?

Living in Reality

Obviously, one not yet acclimated to dwelling in the continuous awareness of what *is* requires some time to become adjusted to perceiving the ordinary world of duality through the nondual perspective. Ultimately, dual and nondual disappear, leaving merely *this*, as it is, nothing more, nothing less.

In more overt ways, life has not changed much. I continue to do almost everything I did before. The difference is that everything is perceived and understood from a different internal perspective. Many chronic emotional issues simply fall away either all at once or gradually. Other issues seem far stickier and require concerted effort to relinquish. Deeply ingrained habits may persist, though certainly not with the same intensity. Most of my adult life I have been something of a workaholic. This pattern is slowly fading, helped along by retirement from my psychotherapy practice in June 2019. The primary difference is that now I usually can observe myself being needlessly driven and still maintain a sense of humor about the issue.

Although I still work hard, everything now occurs on its own. My behavior appears to originate from a commitment to service and gratitude. The inner resistance I once felt to total immersion in the work of this moment is now largely dissolved. When we are fully present for what is, the normal separation between work and the rest of life diminishes. Work, play, rest- everything is just this moment, exactly as it is. It is easier to catch myself overdoing one aspect of my life, and I am more able to back off when needed. Self-judgment and criticism of my perceived failings largely vanished. I can still become irritable when depleted physically or emotionally. Awakening is not the same as sainthood, and I am not a saint! However, most destructive emotional patterns feel much less intrusive and consuming.

Awakening gives us the opportunity to refrain from automatic, conditioned and dysfunctional behavior patterns. We see clearly how painful our previous choices were and lose interest in continuing to be so hurtful to others as well as to ourselves. Still, effort is required until it is not. Eventually effort itself becomes effortless. Although increasingly difficult, it is certainly possible to slip back into grasping for what we do not have or trying to avoid what we do have.

Underneath every second of every day there is an indescribable silent presence, unchanging. Grounded in our moment-to-moment experience, we no longer seek for anything.

What a relief!

Acknowledgements

Infinite gratitude extends to my first Zen teacher Roshi Phillip Kapleau, founder of the Rochester Zen Center, for assisting in the opening of my mind's eye. Deep appreciation also to my second Zen teacher Roshi Bodhin Kjolhede, Roshi Kapleau's Dharma-successor and current Abbot of the Rochester Zen Center in Rochester, New York. All my formal Zen training occurred at this Zen Center. Although I have been deeply influenced by the Zen tradition, I am not a Zen teacher. I only teach and write about what I know directly from my own experience. However, I have found the language of Zen Buddhism, Christianity, and Advaita Vedanta to be helpful in attempting to convey my understanding of direct awareness.

I first discussed the realizations described in this book primarily with my psychotherapy clients. I am grateful for the openness and curiosity with which so many individuals readily embraced these teachings and thereby helped me learn how to articulate them more clearly to others. A consuming question soon emerged after the radical shift in 2002. Why was the direct awareness that was continuous in me and simultaneously equally available to everyone, all the time, not recognized by everyone, automatically? Why are so few of us able to see beyond our self-imposed blinders? The need to answer this question has led to all the teaching and writing I have done since 2002. This book is the result of the need to share my understanding and help explicate how we can facilitate this realization in those who are interested and willing.

My ability to articulate the topics described in this book has been sharpened and clarified by many discussions with Margot Ridler. Margot's ability and willingness to challenge relentlessly whatever sounds *off* to her have been invaluable. She first read the book late in the writing process when I was convinced that it was essentially finished. Substantial rewriting occurred because of her input.

I am grateful to Sister Brigid O'Mahony of the Missionaries of the Heart of Jesus for her weekly Bible study, which has been enormously helpful as well as interesting and inspiring.

I am deeply appreciative of the efforts of everyone who contributed to this project, especially my first editor, Mary Lou Herrick and my current editor, Lynda Helmer.

Thank you everyone.

About the Author

Michael Hall, PhD is a clinical psychologist in Binghamton, New York. He has been engaged in the full-time practice of psychotherapy with individuals, couples, families, and groups for more than forty years.

After graduating from Vanderbilt University in his hometown of Nashville, Tennessee, Michael completed a doctorate in clinical psychology at Indiana University in Bloomington, Indiana. A year-long clinical internship at St. Elizabeth's Hospital, the National Institutes of Mental Health in Washington, D.C., followed. Wanting as much clinical training as possible, he then served two years as a postdoctoral fellow and instructor in clinical psychology in the Department of Psychiatry of the University of Rochester School of Medicine and Dentistry in Rochester, New York. In 1975, Michael began work at the Counseling Center at Binghamton University. Between 1982 and his retirement in 2019, he maintained a full-time private practice in Binghamton, New York.

Michael began to do Zen meditation with a small group of dedicated practitioners in 1978. In 1982 a spontaneous awakening into the formlessness of the physical world occurred after reading the famous lines from The Heart Sutra: *Form here is only emptiness; emptiness only form.* The overwhelming power of this glimpse led to the beginning of serious Zen practice at the Rochester Zen Center, which continued until 1988. Between 1982 and 1984 there were several additional awakening experiences, with recognition of Kensho (seeing one's true nature) by his teacher Roshi Philip Kapleau coming in 1984.

Following his teacher's recommendation, the Zen tradition, and his own appraisal of the limitations of his spiritual understanding, Michael did not speak of his experiences or attempt to share his understanding for twenty years. After an abiding or continuous awareness emerged out of nowhere in 2002, he recognized the end of his searching. In 2005, Michael began sharing his understanding of the spiritual path. He is especially interested in the integration of psychotherapy and spirituality. He shows that the realizations that emerge spontaneously from awakened awareness have a profound effect on how emotional suffering is best understood and treated. Michael focuses on developing effective approaches to alleviating suffering through education and accurate information.

In addition to the application of spiritual awareness to the problems of daily living, Michael is continually aware of emerging opportunities for provoking the shift in consciousness in others who are receptive and willing. His work demonstrates a continuing interest in learning to see reality as it is, rather than how we wish it were or believe it should be.

Michael can be reached at: https://www.DrMichaelHall.com/.

Glossary

There are numerous terms used in this book that may be unfamiliar to you. Even if you have some acquaintance with the words, I may use them in a way that is different from your understanding. This glossary is an attempt to provide brief definitions of some of the primary concepts used in the book, as well as provide context for how I use these terms. Much of the meaning of unfamiliar words can be gleaned from a careful reading of the book, but I believe it will be helpful to describe the major terms here.

Awareness Think of awareness as the ground of being. We normally describe who we are using nouns (man, mother) and adjectives (old, tall, bald). If we leave aside all descriptors, who are you really? In Zen Buddhism this fundamental nature is unchanging and ever present. The great 17th century Zen master Bankei used the term *Unborn* to describe this primordial awareness that is not born and does not die. It is unaffected by the content of awareness, and almost impossible to describe, yet we each experience *it* directly every day. Take away everything you think you are and what is left? Remove every quality and characteristic, and then tell me who you are. We are so identified with and consumed by the content of our mind that we rarely notice the background awareness which contains and notices the content.

When Shakyamuni Buddha, the historical Buddha was asked who he is, he replied *I am awake.* He could have also said *I am awareness.* In Exodus 3:13-15 we find this passage:

> *If I come to the people of Israel and say to them, 'The God of your fathers has sent me to you,' and they ask me, 'What is his name?' what shall I say to them? God said to Moses, 'I AM WHO I AM.' And he said, Say this to the people of Israel, 'I AM has sent me to you.'*

To me this is essentially the same statement as the Buddhas' mentioned above. In John 8: 57-58, Jesus is challenged to clarify who he is, and he replied:

> *So the Jews said to him, 'You are not yet fifty years old, and have you seen Abraham?' Jesus said to them, 'Truly, truly, I say to you, before Abraham was, I am.'*

This *I AM* is the ground of being. It is awareness being fully aware. It is our true nature. It is our purpose in this life to realize this nature and manifest it freely and spontaneously in our behavior.

Awakening This word refers to the recognition of the experiential cessation or ending of the self-creation and improvement project that we are all consumed by under normal circumstances. This direct realization is not an experience when it is deep and thorough. It is consequently impossible to adequately describe, so I and other authors use metaphors and similes. Very similar words include enlightenment and self-realization. I use these terms interchangeably as the subtle differences are not meaningful in this context. The word awakening is used because it feels like waking up from the dream of your life. In 1 Corinthians 13:12 the Apostle Paul, who was literally blinded by the brilliance of direct seeing, describes it:

For now we see only a reflection as in a mirror; then we shall see face to face. Now I know in part; then I shall know fully, even as I am fully known.

Dharma In Buddhism the truth of the Buddhas teaching. This truth is understood to be universal and not contingent on any beliefs or convictions. It is logical, objectively verifiable and does not require or even benefit from holding particular beliefs. It is the same truth regardless of any religious belief or no belief at all. It does not require any prior belief in any concepts to experience directly for yourself. It is the same in all times and places. It is equally available to all human beings, although prodigious work or incredibly good fortune might be necessary to recognize it.

Kensho Within the Japanese Zen tradition Kensho refers to an initial awakening when tested and confirmed by a Zen master. The initial experience can be deep or shallow. The Zen student is required to manifest this understanding spontaneously, without thought, in the presence of the master. A verbal report of a prior experience is not enough. Most kensho experiences in the current era are quite shallow, but capable of infinite deepening. For me kensho occurred during a seven-day silent meditation retreat at the Rochester Zen Center in 1984. I did not speak of it until after the abiding awakening emerged in 2002 because I knew intuitively it was incomplete. Still, kensho represents a massive turning point on the spiritual path.

Nonduality Through a direct, experiential realization we can know for certain that the world as it appears to be is in fact ephemeral, translucent. Nothing is solid or substantial except in terms of appearances. This direct perception of the underlying nature of reality occurred in me spontaneously in 1982. It was the stimulus for my deep commitment to practice and realization of the truth of Buddhist teachings. Since the discoveries of Albert Einstein physicists have known that the objects we perceive as solid are in fact composed of empty space. It is one thing to know it intellectually or through scientific experiments. It is very different to know it experientially.

No-mind This is a Zen Buddhist term that I find useful. I do not know when I first encountered this term, although it is the subject of D. T. Suzuki's book *The Zen Doctrine of No-Mind* (1991). I call it the *other way of knowing* since it refers to a radically different method of accessing information and knowledge about the world and our self. No-mind refers to a knowing field of awareness of infinite potentiality. It represents a completely different way of knowing and being in the world. It can always be accessed, just not by the usual ways of thinking and using our cognitive abilities.

To access this field of knowing requires surrender, trust, and the release of efforts to control our life. This statement is not a belief but a direct experiential knowing. Bert Hellinger, the founder of Family Constellation work, uses the term *knowing field* to describe a somewhat similar, although more limited, phenomena (1998). In the awareness emerging from no-mind, direct knowing occurs spontaneously, seemingly of its own without the conscious mediation of the thinking mind. It is not possible to deliberately make this knowing happen by conscious effort. It appears to occur through grace, although there are ways to make ourselves more accessible to grace. It seems to require a quiet, open and relaxed mind and body to emerge. We are not in charge of its emergence, yet it is readily accessible to everyone, all the time. This topic alone is worthy of an entire book, and more.

Self With a capital *S*, this word refers again to the indescribable awareness of all that both is and is not. The Self is continuously manifest through each of us according to our individual nature. A Zen koan describes it this way: *Show me your original face before your parents were born.* The great 13th century Sufi poet and spiritual teacher Rumi issues the most important challenge we all must face in his wonderful poem *The Great Wagon*:

> *Out beyond ideas of wrongdoing and rightdoing, there is a field.*
> *I'll meet you there.*
>
> The Essential Rumi
New Expanded Edition, 2004

This field is the Self. Rumi took up residence there. We can join him by dropping all ideas of how life, other people and our self should be and seeing everything directly, exactly as it is.

self-identity or self With a small *s* this word represents our ordinary thinking mind or self-identity, who we typically believe we are. We could also use the more psychological term ego here, although self-identity incudes the Freudian concepts of not only ego, but also id and superego. This self is born, lives its' life, and dies. It has a history, is continuous in time and space, and is profoundly conditioned by an infinite number of emotional, physical, biological, cognitive and energetic experiences. It is influenced by the genetics, history, culture, language, nutritional and familial circumstances in which we are born and live.

Life experiences like extensive meditation practice, psychotherapy, accurate spiritual teaching from a trusted source, and supportive social networks can have a markedly beneficial impact on the self. Virtually all self-help books and efforts directed towards self-improvement are aimed at the betterment of the self. A healthier, happier self is often attainable through skillful and persistent effort and is certainly worth the work involved. Liberation from suffering cannot be achieved in this manner. It can only occur through the thorough recognition and embodiment of the Self.

True nature This term refers to who we really are underneath all social conditioning and programming. See the previous descriptions of *Awareness* and the *Self,* as there is considerable overlap in the meaning of these terms. Conceptual thought, language, logic, and rational thinking can provide a description of who we fundamentally are, but all words fail to convey the power of the living presence of one who is awake to their true nature. Nothing can be either added or removed from it. It is whole and complete just as it is. So are all of us in our essential nature.

Vasana A Sanskrit term used primarily in Advaita Vedanta to describe ingrained, habitual tendencies which are largely unconscious. Some vasanas may be socially beneficial, such as an inner drive or compulsion to work hard and be conscientious. Other vasanas are clearly dysfunctional and are the subject matter of psychotherapy and other efforts at self-improvement, such as 12-step groups. We all have many of these habit patterns and rooting them out is a long process. It is important work that occurs both before and after awakening. In a deep and abiding awakening, many of these habit patterns are vaporized instantaneously and without effort, never to return. Other vasanas linger and endure indefinitely until directly acknowledged, confronted and released through diligent effort and insight.

Although I have met quite a few people who have had some degree of awakening, I have never personally met anyone who was completely free of these ingrained habits. As long as we have a human body and mind, there will be blind spots. My personal experience, as well as my experience guiding spiritual students, is that it is easier to see your own blind spots before a deep awakening. There are many reasons for this that are beyond the scope of this discussion.

I have found it to be very difficult to even see, much less release, highly defended, ego syntonic patterns of behavior. The only way that has worked for me is to have either a trusted spiritual teacher or very close, wise and perceptive friend point out these patterns. Usually these pointing's must happen repeatedly. Even then resistance and denial are problematic. Apologies all around! We are all a work in progress. No one currently alive, as far as I know, has finished this psychic excavation. I do not, however, want to make this work seem grim or overwhelming. With spiritual, energetic, physical and psychological effort, enormous progress will occur. There is also a Princess and the pea phenomenon. The issues and work involved gradually become more subtle and daily life much more enjoyable and far less problematic. Part of the difficulty is that many resistant patterns are biologically based, and intrinsic to our animal nature. Many others are virtually universal for men; others occur mostly in women. Humility is essential, and a sense of humor very helpful. This is the subject of another book.

Resources

There are an enormous number of very helpful resources available online and in bookstores now that were simply not available when I began the spiritual quest in 1965. At that time, I searched for books in the Vanderbilt University library and found virtually nothing that could assist me. What I did find was some original source material, primarily the *Upanishads* and the *Bhagavad Gita*. Paramahansa Yogananda's *Autobiography of a Yogi* was available, but I did not discover it until ten years later. There was also a Buddhism journal *The Middle Way* edited by Christmas Humphries from England, and Evelyn Underhill's wonderful book *Mysticism: A Study in the Nature and Development of Spiritual Consciousness*, originally published in 1911.

Perhaps the most useful book was assigned as required reading in my Phenomenology of Religion course with Professor Winston King that I talked my way into my junior year in college. It was necessary to convince Professor King of my serious intent because I had no prerequisites in religion, and it was a graduate level course. All the other students in the small class were in the Divinity School or graduate school pursuing PhDs in Philosophy or Religion. The book was *The Heart of Buddhist Meditation*: *A Handbook of Mental Training Based On The Buddha's Way Of Mindfulness* (1962) by Nyanaponika Thera. This excellent book described in detail mindfulness meditation practices of the Theravadin Buddhism of Burma and Southeast Asia. This was tremendously helpful as it gave me a practice-something to *do*.

Reading and conceptualizing can only take you so far. By 1967 my future teacher Roshi Philip Kapleau's seminal book *The Three Pillars of Zen* was published. It also provided detailed instruction on how to practice sitting meditation according to the Zen tradition he learned in his 13 years of practice in Japanese monasteries and temples beginning in the early 1950s. The way of Zen seemed challenging but possible for me, and there was a native English-speaking American teacher available in Rochester, New York. I settled in for the long haul.

Life itself, with resources both seen and unseen, rises to support a serious intention on the spiritual path. You do not need to be concerned about finding appropriate resources to support your search. Life will provide whatever you need if liberation is your heart's desire. It is all so finely tuned as to be incomprehensible to a mind conditioned to believe that it oversees and is in charge of what happens. Ask God, the Universe, the Self, Emptiness or the Source of All that Is for guidance on the best path for you, and you will be shown what you need. This asking does not require any preexisting belief. A willingness to be guided by an unknown, undefined Higher Power is all you need. This, of course, is where many people get stuck, as they do with the first step in Alcoholics Anonymous where recognition of our powerlessness over addiction is acknowledged. It is fine to not know where to go or how to begin. Simply ask in a sincere, humble manner to be guided to the path that is most resonant with your being, and it will happen.

In terms of suggestions, I can only share what seemed to benefit me or others I trust and know well. Here are a few ideas:

Ashrams Although not my personal lineage, many ashrams and teaching centers exist in North America and abroad that provide training in the Advaita Vedanta teaching, a nondual variant of contemporary Hinduism. As in Buddhism there are many lineages and schools. One of the most famous and accessible is *Transcendental Meditation* popularized in this country by Maharishi Mahesh Yogi in the late 1960s, and widely available today.

Chanting Chanting is a key spiritual practice in most traditional religions, and it was certainly an important component of Zen training. It is best to receive some basic chanting instruction and is easiest when done as part of a group.

Contemplative Prayer Contemplation has long been one of the core Catholic spiritual practices, which also include repetitive prayer, such as the *Our Father* and *Hail Mary*, as well as the *Stations of the Cross* and meditating on scripture (*Lectio Divina*). Father Thomas Keating and several of his Benedictine brothers helped resurrect contemplative prayer in the 1970s. His lovely book *Intimacy with God* (2009) gives an excellent overview of these traditional practices.

Ecstatic Dance Popularized by the Indian teacher Osho in the 1970s and 80s, ecstatic dance is described as free form movement, without judgment or restriction. Many people, perhaps especially women, do not resonate with silent meditation or the moving meditation of yoga or the martial arts. Rhythmic, free form dance can be a liberating way out of the prison of your mind and its constricted patterns of thought.

Marital Arts Like yoga, there are an infinite number of approaches to the traditional martial arts, including Karate, Aikido, Tai Chi, Chi Kung, Judo, Taekwondo, Jujitsu and others. I trained in a Japanese/Okinawan martial art for 15 years. These practices condition, relax and strengthen body and mind. Most are also infused with an appreciation of Chi, the life force energy that permeates all living beings. They also teach self-defense, with the preference always being for nonviolence and harm avoidance when possible.

Mindfulness Meditation Centers Mindfulness training is common to all schools of Buddhism but has been most identified with the Vipassana or Theravadin schools that emerged in Southeast Asia, especially Burma, Laos, Cambodia, and Sri Lanka. Training in mindfulness is an excellent foundation to other forms of meditation practices, as it focuses on paying careful attention to the facts of our moment-to-moment experience.

Shamanism While certainly not for everyone, I personally benefitted from long practice and training in shamanism. Like most of the approaches mentioned above, shamanism works with various energy bodies, such as the astral and etheric bodies in order to facilitate healing and to cleanse and purify energy. One of the primary benefits for me was directly experiencing repeatedly the nonlocality of consciousness. It became normal for me to leave my physical body in order to do shamanic work. Shamanism as well as other therapeutic energy work, such as Thought Field Therapy, Emotional Freedom techniques, and EMDR, all of which I was trained to perform before my awakening in 2002, seemed to help prepare the way for the occurrence of the enduring cessation of becoming.

The Jesus Prayer The prayer is *Lord Jesus Christ, Son of God, have mercy on me, a sinner*. Widely utilized in the Eastern Orthodox Christian tradition, the Jesus Prayer is often repeated in coordination with the breath. A contemporary practitioner, who has written extensively of his experience, is the English mystic John Butler.

Tibetan Centers Tibetan Buddhism, along with Zen, is a part of Mahayana Buddhism. While my own experience with Tibetan Buddhism is limited, I feel a deep personal resonance with this tradition. There are many Tibetan monasteries and teaching centers around the world, especially in India, Europe and the Americas. Tibetan Buddhism is historically associated not only with greater Tibet, including Sichuan and other parts of China, but also with Inner and Outer Mongolia, Bhutan, and parts of southern Siberia.

Yoga Training in many forms of yoga are widely available and would be helpful in addition to other approaches to meditation. Yoga is routinely taught at most ashrams as well as yoga studios and is easily accessible virtually anywhere. Yogic approaches to breath training or pranayama, are enormously helpful to any meditation practice. The coordination of stretching, breathing and relaxation help prepare the stiff Western body, accustomed to inactivity with poor posture and breathing, for long periods of silent meditation. Some training in yoga is invaluable for any meditation practice.

Zen Centers There are Zen Centers throughout the United States and Europe. They provide serious training in meditation and Mahayana Buddhism for those who have a sincere aspiration and are willing to work. There is nothing lax or easy about training in an authentic Zen Center, but who said disciplining an unruly mind was going to be easy? The Rochester Zen Center in Rochester, New York can be easily found online at rzc.org. There are affiliated Zen Centers around the United States and Canada, Europe, Mexico and New Zealand. There are many other Zen Buddhist organizations around the world that provide training and teaching in Buddhism. Zen is a school of Buddhism which originally flourished in China, Korea, Thailand and Japan.

BOOKS

One purpose of the bibliography in this book is to provide a list of books that I have found helpful. Approximately twenty of the books are primarily focused on psychological issues. All the rest discuss different approaches to spiritual development. Some are grounded in traditional religions, but many are not. In all books that seem oriented towards a religious approach, the author stresses the meditative or mystical aspects. Some of the books may seem difficult to grasp for those new to the spiritual search, but all are useful. When I was in college I would disappear into the stacks of the vast library and read whatever seemed to fall into my hands. I tended to read only what interested me, making my academic record a bit uneven. I recommend this method for those who are sufficiently open to the guidance of

Life. Assume that *something* knows what is best for you at any given time. This something cannot be defined but is nevertheless very real. *It* is the unseen force in the universe which makes everything happen. *It* knows far better than our thinking minds what would be ideal at this moment to read. Do not make reading or any other aspect of this path into a problem. If you start to read something and it does not seem to grab you or resonate, let it go. It probably is not what you currently need. Learn to look for and trust this unseen *knowing field*. This universe is infinitely more mysterious and wonderful than we realize. There are always powerful forces seen and unseen supporting our search.

VIDEOS

Regarding useful information freely available on the internet, we live in the best of times and the worst of times, to paraphrase the famous lines from the opening paragraph of Charles Dickens *A Tale of Two Cities*. The worst of times because it is possible to watch so many videos and read so many books that a false belief arises that you understand nondual reality because you are familiar with the concepts. Far better to sit quietly, doing nothing much, just sitting, allowing the body and mind to rest. Or go for a walk in nature, or do almost any physical activity, including yoga, ecstatic dance, exercise, and so forth. The main idea is to get your attention away from your thoughts, which are usually ruminations, worries, and fantasies, and into your body and actual real experience.

We live in the best of times because there are a multitude of excellent videos posted, especially on YouTube, Vimeo and Facebook. I have channels on all these streaming platforms, and you are welcome to check out my pages.

Vimeo: https://vimeo.com/michaelhallphd
YouTube: www.youtube.com/user/perceptionisall/videos
Facebook: https://www.facebook.com/MichaelHallPhD/

In addition to my own videos, I recommend any of David Godman's videos on YouTube about Ramana Maharshi and the other great 20th century Indian teachers, including Nisargadatta Maharaj, Papaji, Ramesh Balsekar, and others. Godman is the long-time librarian for Ramana Maharshi's ashram in Tiruvannamalai, India, and is an excellent historian and communicator. The teachings of Ramana Maharshi and his students offer a very high level of revealed truth and are readily available in books and videos. Many contemporary Western teachers trace their lineage to these great 20th century Indian teachers.

As I mentioned in the previous section on books, it is fine to open a streaming platform like YouTube and explore videos available under the topic of spiritual enlightenment or spiritual awakening. You will need to develop some discernment to recognize what might be most helpful to you, as there are many videos which are basically infomercials. Still, trial and error are the nature of the spiritual search. Trust yourself to find what you need.

Bibliography

Adyashanti. (2009). *The End of Your World: Uncensored Straight Talk on the Nature of Enlightenment.* Boulder, CO: Sounds True.

Aitkin, R. (Trans.). (2003). *A Zen Wave: Basho's Haiku and Zen.* New York: Shoemaker & Hoard.

Alcoholics Anonymous Big Book (4thed). (2001). New York: Alcoholics Anonymous.

Appelbaum, S. (Ed.). (1992). *The Rime of the Ancient Mariner.* Mineola, NY: Dover.

Balsekar, R. (1999). *Who Cares?! The Unique Teaching of Ramesh S. Balsekar.* Redondo Beach, CA.

Berry, W. (1987). *The Collected Poems of Wendell Berry, 1957-1982.* Albany, CA: North Point.

Bill W. *Spiritual Experiences.* (1992, July). *The International Journal of Alcoholics Anonymous,* 19. Retrieved April 1, 2008 from the AA Grapevine, Inc. digital archive.

Blofeld, J. (Ed.). (1958). *The Zen Teaching of Huang Po on the Transmission of Mind.* New York: Grove.

Blofeld, J. (Trans.). (2007). *Ch'an Master Hui Hai. Zen Teaching of Instantaneous Awakening.* Devon, UK: Buddhist Publishing Group.

Brunton, Paul. (1984). *Perspectives: The Timeless Way of Wisdom (Posthumous). Vol. One. The Notebooks of Paul Brunton.* Burdett, NY: Larson Publications.

Butler, John. (2008). *Wonders of Spiritual Unfoldment.* London: Shepheard-Walwyn.

Caplan, M. (1999). *Halfway Up the Mountain: The Error of Premature Claims of Enlightenment.* Prescott, AZ: Holm.

Carnes, P. (1997). *The Betrayal Bond. Breaking Free of Exploitive Relationships.* Deerfield Beach, FL: Health Publications.

Carnes, P., with Morarity, J. (1997) *Sexual Anorexia: Overcoming Sexual Self-hatred.* Center City, MN: Hazelden.

Chants and Recitations. (2005). Rochester, NY: Rochester Zen Center.

Csikszentmihalyi, M. (2008). *Flow: The Psychology of Optimal Experience.* New York: Harper.

Davies, S. (2003). *The Gospel of Thomas: Annotated and explained.* Woodstock, VT: Skylight Paths.

Ehrman, B.D. (2008). *God's Problem. How the Bible fails to answer our most important questions-why we suffer.* New York: HarperCollins.

Eliot, T.S. (1980). *The Complete Poems and Plays: 1909-1950.* Orlando, FL: Harcourt, Brace.

Gendlin, E. (1998). *Focusing-Oriented Psychotherapy: A Manual of the Experiential Method.* New York: Guilford.

Godman, D. (Ed.). (1992). *Be As You Are*: *The Teachings of Sri Ramana Maharshi.* New York: Penguin.

Godman, D. (Ed.). (1998). *Nothing Ever Happened.* Boulder, CO: Avadhuta Foundation.

Gorrell, D.L. (2001). *Perfect Madness: From Awakening to Enlightenment.* Maui, HI: Inner Ocean.

Griffin, E. (Ed.). (2004). *John of the Cross: Selections from the Dark Night and other writings.* New York: HarperCollins.

Hakuin. *Master Hakuin's Chant in Praise of Zazen.* (2005). *Chants and Recitations.* Rochester, NY: Rochester Zen Center.

Hawkins, D. (2002). *Power vs. Force: The Hidden Determinants of Human Behavior.* Carlsbad, CA: Hay House.

Hellinger, B., Weber, G., and Beaumont, H. (1998). *Love's Hidden Symmetry: What Makes Love Work in Relationships.* Phoenix: Zeig Tucker & Theisen Inc.

Johnston, W. (Ed.) (1996). *The Cloud of Unknowing and the Book of Privy Counseling.* New York: Doubleday, Image Books.

Kapleau, Roshi P. (1980). *The Three Pillars of Zen*. Garden City, New York: Anchor.

Katie, B, and Mitchell, S. (2002). *Loving What Is: Four Questions that can Change your Lives*. New York: Three Rivers.

Keating, T. (2009). *Intimacy with God: An Introduction to Centering Prayer*. Third Edition. New York: The Crossroad Publishing Company.

King, W. (1962). *A Thousand Lives Away: Buddhism in Contemporary Burma*. Cambridge, Mass: Harvard University.

Kolodiejchuk, B. (Ed.). (2007). *Mother Teresa: Come be my Light. The private writings of the "Saint of Calcutta"*. New York: Doubleday.

Levinson, H. N., with Carter, S. (1988). *Phobia Free: Medical breakthrough linking 90% of all phobias and panic attacks to a hidden physical problem*. New York: M. Evans.

Low, A (1990). *The World; A Gateway. Commentaries on the Mumonkan*. Rutland, VT: Tuttle.

Low, A. (2000). *Zen and the Sutras*. Boston: Tuttle.

Low, A. (Ed.). (2006). *Hakuin on Kensho. The Four Ways of Knowing*. Boston: Shambala.

Mair, V.H. (1990). *Tao Te Ching*. New York: Bantam.

Marshall, B. (2009). *The Perennial Way*. Wheeling, WV: TAT Foundation.

Masters, R.A. (2010). *Spiritual Bypassing: When spirituality disconnects us from what really matters*. Berkeley, CA: North Atlantic.

McKenna, J. (2002). *Spiritual Enlightenment: The Damnedest Thing*. Wisefool Press.

Melody, P. (2003). *Facing Love Addiction: Giving yourself the power to change the way you love*. New York: Harper One.

Melody, P. (2003). *Facing Codependence: What it is, where it comes from, how it sabotages our lives*. New York: Harper One.

Nadeen, S. (2000). *From Seekers to Finders: The Myth and Reality about Enlightenment*. Conyers, GA: New Freedom.

Nyanaponika Thera (1962). *The Heart of Buddhist Meditation: A Handbook of Mental Training Based On The Buddha's Way Of Mindfulness*. London: Rider & Company.

Packer, T. (2000). *The Wonder of Presence: And the Way of Meditative Inquiry*. Boston: Shambala.

Pagels, E. (2003). *Beyond Belief: The Secret Gospel of Thomas*. New York: Random House.

Pennebaker, J. and Evans, J. (2014). *Expressive Writing: Words that Heal*. Enumclaw, WA: Idyll Arbor.

Pine, R. (1987). *The Zen Teaching of Bodhidharma*. New York: North Point.

Pokrovsky, G. (2001). Harvey, A., Forward. *The Way of a Pilgrim: The Jesus Prayer Journey—Annotated & Explained*. Woodstock, VT: Skylight Illuminations.

Ramaji, and Ananda Devi. (2014) *1000: The Levels of Consciousness and a Map of the Stages of Awakening for Spiritual Seekers and Teachers*. San Diego: Rasa Transmission International Books.

Ridler, M. (eBook). (2019). *True Freedom versus Self-Improvement: A Life Without Suffering Can Be Yours*.

Rose, R. (2001). *Psychology of the Observer*. McMechen, WV: TAT Foundation.

Rogers, C., and Kramer, P. (1995). *On Becoming a Person: A Therapist's View of Psychotherapy*. New York: Mariner Books.

Ruiz, D. M. (1997). *The Four Agreements*. San Rafael, CA: Amber-Allen.

Rumi, Jalal al-Din (Author), Barks, C. (Translator), Moyne, J. (Translator) (2004). *The Essential Rumi, New Expanded Edition*. New York: Harper One.

Sarno, J. E. (1998). *The Mindbody Prescription: Healing the Body, Healing the Pain*. New York: Warner.

Segal, S. (1996). *Collision with the Infinite: A Life Beyond the Personal Self.* San Diego, CA: Blue Dove.

Seng-ts'an. *Affirming Faith in Mind.* (2005). In *Chants and Recitations.* Rochester, NY: Rochester Zen Center.

Sekito Kisen. (2005). *The Harmony of Relative and Absolute (Sandokai),* in *Chants and Recitations.* Rochester, NY: Rochester Zen Center.

Sogyal Rinpoche. (1994). *The Tibetan Book of Living and Dying.* (P. Gaffney & A. Harvey, Eds.). New York: HarperCollins.

Soko Morinaga. (1988). *The Ceasing of Notions. A Zen Text from the Tun-Huang caves.* London: The Zen Centre.

Taylor, J. B. (2008). *My Stroke of Insight: A brain scientist's personal journey.* New York: Viking.

Thompson, Charles. (1990). *The Thompson chain reference Bible. Second improved edition: New international version.* Indianapolis, IN: B. B. Kirkbride Bible Co.

Thorburn, D. (2001). *Drunks, Drugs & Debits: How to recognize Addicts and avoid financial abuse.* Northridge, CA: Galt.

Thoreau, H.D. (2004). Cramer, J.S. (Ed.). *Walden: A fully annotated edition.* New Haven: Yale University.

Tolle, E. (1999). *The Power of Now: A Guide to Spiritual Enlightenment.* Novato, CA: New World Library.

Underhill, Evelyn. (2017). *Mysticism: A Study in the Nature and Development of Spiritual Consciousness.* Lebanon, New Jersey: Franklin Classics.

Wolf, Naomi. (2002). *The Beauty Myth: How Images of Beauty Are Used Against Women.* New York: Harper Perennial.

Made in the USA
San Bernardino, CA
19 January 2020